Praise for *Craving Grace*

Ruth Delk has given us one of the most incredibly faithful, creative, and accessible books on God's grace I've ever read. *Craving Grace* is a veritable show-and-tell of God's commitment to do for us in Jesus what we could never do for ourselves—bring redemption, joy, and freedom to our lives. This little book is a Trojan horse of understanding about the only love that will never let us go—the only love that is enough to meet the deepest cravings and longings of our hearts.

—SCOTTY SMITH *Founding Pastor of Christ Community Church, author of* Everyday Prayers: 365 Days to a Gospel Centered Faith; Objections of His Affection; The Reign of Grace; Restoring Broken Things

How on earth did she do that? Ruthie Delk has taken 10,000 complex problems and reduced them down to a single diagram. This book presents the clearest explanation of how grace and sanctification work that I've ever read. No matter where you are on your journey, this book should definitely be on your "must read" list. You're going to love *Craving Grace*.

—PATRICK MORLEY, PHD *Author, Founder and Chairman, Man in the Mirror*

My best friend gave me the book *Craving Grace*. While I have been a Christian for many years, and a missionary, I found that this book explained the gospel in such a way, that I realized it was not stale, old news, but fresh, appreciated, vital news—needed every day for my walk with God. Recently, my husband and I lost our 16-year-old son. I can honestly say that the truths Ruthie reminded me of in a poignant and clear way have been used by God during this time of grieving and suffering, as day by day we come to Him and are amazed at what He has provided for us, because of what Jesus did on the cross, to give us the strength and power to make it through the day.

—KATIE S

During a lonely time, when I could sense depression setting in, *Craving Grace* inspired me to look at the gospel in such a way that I fell deeply in love with my Savior all over again. My circumstances didn't change, but my heart did. Ruthie's honest words both challenged me and convicted me.

—CONNIE R

Ruthie has created a profound, relevant and surprisingly simple diagram that illustrates the beauty and mystery of our kinship to Jesus. We belong to Him, yet the wounds and false beliefs of our stories leave us orphaned and alone. May the truth of the Gospel Eight soak into my heart and mind as well as into the clients God brings into my counseling office, and anyone who is fortunate enough to read this book. Thank you, Ruthie, for a transformative work about who we were meant to be at the core of our being.

—RACHEL BLACKSTON, MA, MEd. *Licensed Mental Health Counselor, Redeemer Counseling*

With its memorable visual framework and incredibly accurate portraits of the human heart, *Craving Grace* shapes my thinking long after I put the book aside. I feel that I now understand to a much greater degree how to actually apply the mind-boggling truth of the gospel to my everyday life. This is one of those books that is so powerful, it should be read at least once a year!

—MICHELE D

Craving Grace is a conceptual masterpiece. Ruthie's simple step-by-step Gospel Eight diagram brilliantly breaks down the attributes of God, our relationship with Him, the impact of our choices, and the power of His love and grace. As a mental health counselor, I recommend this book in my practice as a must-read to clients of all ages.

—HEIDI M. JACKSON, MA *Owner of the Center for Family & Crisis Counseling, Orlando, FL*

EXPERIENCE THE RICHNESS OF THE GOSPEL

RUTHIE DELK

MOODY PUBLISHERS
CHICAGO

Published in association with the literary agency of Wolgemuth & Associates, Inc., 8600 Crestgate Circle, Orlando, Florida 32819.

Edited by Annette LaPlaca
Cover and interior design: Smartt Guys design
Cover photo: Nils Z/iStock
Author photo: Rachel M. Whited
Gospel Eight diagram © 2014 by Ruthie Delk

Library of Congress Cataloging-in-Publication Data

Delk, Ruthie.
Craving grace : experience the richness of the gospel / Ruthie Delk.
pages cm
Includes bibliographical references.
ISBN 978-0-8024-1124-2
1. Grace (Theology) I. Title.
BT761.3.D45 2014
234--dc23

2013036632

We hope you enjoy this book from Moody Publishers. Our goal is to provide high-quality, thought-provoking books and products that connect truth to your real needs and challenges. For more information on other books and products written and produced from a biblical perspective, go to www.moodypublishers.com or write to:

Moody Publishers
820 N. LaSalle Boulevard
Chicago, IL 60610

3 5 7 9 10 8 6 4 2

Printed in the United States of America

CONTENTS

It is good for our hearts to be strengthened by grace.

HEBREWS 13:9

WHY THIS BOOK?

Since you are reading this book, it means a piece of my heart has found its way into your hands. Frankly, I'm humbled by the thought. My prayer is that this Gospel Eight diagram and the accompanying pages will open your heart to see the gospel in a new way.

There are no earth-shattering truths here. You won't read anything that hasn't been said before by people far better read and theologically savvy than I. This is simply the fruit of my journey—a journey where God breathed life into what had become sterile and meaningless to me.

Can you believe I would say that about the gospel? *Sterile and meaningless?* Twenty years ago those exact words would have perfectly described the impact and importance of the gospel in my life.

At that point I could have recited a list of accomplishments that would have rivaled Paul's in Philippians. I became a Christian when I was a child and was raised in a Christian home (as a missionary kid to be exact—there must be extra points for that!). By the time I was a young adult, I knew all the answers (at least I thought I did) and was an expert in keeping pace on my spiritual treadmill.

If this is true, why isn't it making a difference in my life?

During high school and college I had a dog-eared copy of *Pursuit of Holiness* by Jerry Bridges. It was pretty much my bible. I kept copies to give away and was determined that holiness was within reach, if I just tried hard enough.

But while my husband, David, was in seminary (perfect timing, right?), I had a faith crisis that revealed a disconnect between my head and my heart. This agonizing question kept ringing in my ears: *If **this** is really true then why isn't it making a difference in my life—in how I handle disappointment, how I deal with my pain, how I parent, how I relate to my husband, and on and on?*

I was at the point of spiritual exhaustion. If someone had told me to DO one more thing, I think I would have thrown up. **Seriously!** I was so tired of going through the motions, but I was caught on a performance treadmill. I felt completely stuck. I was craving something more. I just had no idea what.

I believed the gospel had the power to change people; it

just wasn't changing me. And I was miserable. This disconnect showed up in questions like these:

> *If I believed God's love was unconditional, why did I feel loved on the days I "got it right" and feel abandoned on the days I "got it wrong"?*
>
> *If I really believed God was in control, why was I so fearful?*
>
> *If I really believed He was with me, why did I feel so alone?*
>
> *If I really believed His grace saved and forgave me, why couldn't I extend that same grace to others?*

My head was filled with brilliant knowledge about all the wonderful attributes of God, but my heart was not convinced He even knew my name.

During this time, as only God could orchestrate, Jerry Bridges showed up at the seminary to teach on his book *Transforming Grace*. David, knowing how much I loved *Pursuit of Holiness* and also how much I was struggling with my faith, encouraged me to attend. I look back now and know without a doubt that God used that class and book to introduce me to grace and breathe life back into me.

Ironically, as I write this, Jerry Bridges has just released his book *The Transforming Power of the Gospel*. In an interview recently, he said this about his growth in the gospel: "My first book, *The Pursuit of Holiness*, became a bestseller. But I soon realized that a pursuit of holiness that is not founded on grace and the gospel can lead to a performance mentality and even to discouragement. That's when I began to emphasize grace and the gospel as foundational to the pursuit of holiness."[1]

I desperately needed to be rescued from that performance mentality and discouragement! While I was taking that class, I discovered I didn't **really** grasp grace or the gospel. I knew about it in my head but was not experiencing it in my heart. **I felt dead inside.** The truncated gospel I believed in **was** sterile and meaningless. Why? *Primarily because my definition of the gospel was so limited.* The gospel I believed in was sterile and meaningless.

At that time if you asked me what the gospel was, I would have rattled off the typical answer that it is the good news, or I'd have shown you a colorfully beaded bracelet that told you a story about your sin and the solution to it. End of story. That was it. The gospel was simply the entry point. It was the way to begin a relationship with God. Then it was time to go to work. Yes, I believed God saved me, but sanctification (the part about growing and becoming more like Christ)—that was up to me.

Over time my definition of the gospel deepened, and it changed my view of God as well as my view of sin. An expanding view of God's *holiness*, *love*, and *grace* seeped into my heart and created a growing awareness of my own sin. This made me really uncomfortable but at the same time revealed what was going on in my heart. I realized I had been making the gospel small. Why?

Because if I didn't need a big gospel or a big Jesus, then I didn't have to face up to being a big sinner. The pattern looked something like this:

When confronted by failure or inadequacy,
I minimized my sin, which led to . . .

Minimizing the holiness of God, which led to . . .

Believing in a small God, a small Jesus, a small cross,
and a big self.

I found the inverse of this was also true: a small view of Jesus and a small view of God led to a small view of my sin.

No wonder the gospel wasn't changing me! As the true gospel became clearer to me, I began to see that . . .

A big view of my sin led to . . .

A big view of the holiness of God, which meant that . . .

I started worshiping a big God, a big Jesus, a big cross,
and believing in a smaller self.

When I started sharing what I was experiencing, I quickly learned I was not alone. I was surrounded by an army of gospel "tweakers." But we are not the first generation to water down the gospel. In Galatians 1:6–7 Paul warned his readers by saying, "I am astonished that you are so quickly deserting the one who called you to live in the **grace** of Christ and are turning to a **different** gospel—which is **really no gospel at all** (emphasis added)."

Peter wrote, "So I will always remind you of these things, even though you know them and are firmly established in the truth you now have. I think it is right to refresh your memory... I will make every effort to see that after my departure you will always be able to **remember** these things" (2 Peter 1:12–15, emphasis added).

This is why I need to be *reminded* of the gospel. You do, too. We are, as the old hymn states, "prone to wander . . . prone to leave the God [we] love."[2] We need to remember the true gospel—**the one based on His work, not ours. The gospel that changes everything.**

The first time I heard the phrase *Preach the gospel to yourself every day*, I was dumbfounded. I had no clue what that meant. In my mind I envisioned myself pulling out one of the colorful beaded gospel bracelets and reciting the plan of salvation several times a day. I had a lot to learn. I'm thankful God surrounded me with a Christian community and friends who were wrestling with these same issues.

As I grappled with what it looked like in real life to "preach the gospel to myself," I knew I needed a visual to help me understand the tug-of-war between faith and unbelief going on in my heart. How could I make sense of the way I was living like a spiritual orphan and His child almost simultaneously? As the diagram in this book evolved, it helped me get a handle on the driving force behind my spiritual split personality.

The Gospel Eight diagram and the description that follows is simply a tool to remind us of the gospel. *The real gospel*. The gospel that brings freedom and life and hope. A gospel worth celebrating and sharing! *The gospel that changes everything!*

I am especially grateful to family and friends, who have shared with me, cried with me, encouraged me, and challenged me all along this journey. This diagram has been tweaked and modified as every Bible study group has improved it and made it a truer reflection of the cycle of faith in action. I am pretty sure this diagram is still not in its final stage. As I grow in my own understanding of the gospel, it will change. *Like any illustration, it can't say everything that needs to be said. It is just meant to start the conversation.*

My prayer is that this diagram will do for you what it has done for me: give you a clear and concrete way *to preach the gospel to yourself every day*. I hope the diagram will give you a way to find yourself in this story and help you see clearly how much God loves you, how the cross is the answer to your sin, how His grace propels you on the journey, and how the gospel can bring healing to the hurting places of your heart.

I also pray the diagram will be a useful resource you can share with others, to show them how Christ really is the answer to everything.

Let's get started! I can't wait to share my journey with you.

1

THE GOSPEL EVERY DAY

The **gospel** is the doorway to our salvation, the essential truths we need to believe about Jesus in order to be saved. And yet it is also much, much, more! **It's not just the doorway; it's also the pathway.** It is every promise, every fact, every attribute of God, and everything we need to know, understand, and experience about God and His grace. As described in Ephesians 1, the gospel encompasses every spiritual blessing that we have in Christ. That's why the word *gospel* literally means *good news*. Indeed it is!

Child of God
RESTORATION
DEFINED BY
He is... I am...
forgiver forgiven
Redeemer redeemed
Savior healer saved healed
provider provided for
defender defended
lover loved
Rest in the Gospel? Will I or Resist
REPENT

RESIST
DEFINED BY
• PAIN • PAST
• CIRCUMSTANCES
I was... I am...
rejected bitter
abused lonely
controlled controlling
judged afraid
hurt angry

MINIMIZING
CONTEMPT
BLAMING
DENIAL
FALSE REPENTANCE

ISOLATION

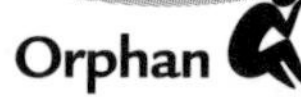
Orphan

#1
Approval
Work
Family
$$$
FALSE GODS

A QUICK **OVERVIEW** of the GOSPEL EIGHT

The Gospel Eight diagram reflects what the process of repenting and believing looks like in our lives. This is a fluid process, and so you will notice little arrows that indicate movement around the diagram. These arrows represent God's grace and His relentless pursuit of us. You will also notice that, no matter where you might be "standing" in this diagram, His grace is always propelling you, moving you back into relationship with Him.

Looking at the diagram, you can see there really is no beginning and no end. Since it's a cycle and a process, anywhere you start will be "jumping in midstream." But we have to start somewhere, so let's begin with the top part of the diagram that reflects the ideal of a believer's relationship with God as Father. As Christians, we enjoy all the spiritual blessings offered to us in the gospel. As His children, our identity is based on who He is, not who we are. Secure in the Father's love, we delight in sharing with others and inviting them to join the journey. The diagram has no beginning and no end; it's a cycle and a process.

Even as His children, we fail miserably. If I'm honest, I know I'm constantly confronted with my inadequacy and sin. Like a mirror, God uses His Word, the Holy Spirit, and the community of believers to expose my unbelief and the way sin has power over me.

Burdened by this reality, the intersection of the two circles reflects the choice where we decide what we will do with the growing awareness of our sin and the accompanying shame and pain it brings. How will I respond when I feel the weight of my sin? I can repent and run to the cross, or I can resist and turn away from the cross.

Rest in the Gospel or Resist Will I

In repentance I find full forgiveness that restores me to an intimate fellowship with God. Some have referred to this top portion of the diagram as the Cycle of Faith—a repetitive cycle of repenting and believing, repenting and believing. **This is preaching the gospel to yourself.**

Oh, if only it were this easy! Unfortunately, my heart is easily derailed. Perhaps Satan plants a seed of doubt large enough to make me suspicious of God and His intentions for me. Or maybe I simply mistrust God's plan. Or maybe I just feel like I'm not really that bad. For whatever reason, I convince myself I can handle my sin and my pain on my own and don't really need Him.

Although I am aware of my sin and brokenness, I bypass the cross, resist repentance, and instead head down a path of false repentance that leads me away from God (and into the bottom circle of the diagram).

On this downward path, I develop clever schemes to "manage my sin." From the outside, managing my sin can look like repentance, but it's not. It's false repentance.

False repentance is looking to something else to take away the shame, guilt, and consequences of my sin.

I might do this by blame-shifting, beating myself up, denying my sin, minimizing my sin, or trying to "fix it" on my own by self-effort and trying harder. But all of these lead me further away from God. I *feel* more and more isolated and separated from Him. I end up living a life more characteristic of a spiritual orphan than God's child.[1]

Instead of finding my identity in Christ and what He has done for me, as in the top circle, my identity as a spiritual orphan is defined by my pain, my past, and my circumstances. Life as an orphan robs me of hope, freedom, acceptance, and joy. It leaves me with precisely the life Satan would have me live—one that is disconnected from Christ and that feels spiritually sterile and wearisome.

As a result, since I've rejected the righteousness that Christ

> Idols are a cheap substitute for Christ; they all disappoint in the end.

has given me, I strive to establish my own (like the Israelites, Romans 10:3). I do this by propping myself up with anything that gives me value and fulfills my need for acceptance. The Bible calls these things idols.

Idols are a cheap substitute for Christ. They may work for a little while, but they all disappoint in the end. At some point I realize these idols don't deliver and are actually sucking the life out of me. They are driving me further from Christ and the life He intended. Once again, like a mirror, God's Word, the Holy Spirit, and the community of faith help me realize my brokenness and my need for a Savior.

Now I face the same choice. I can run to the cross and be restored through repentance and faith, or I can resist the cross and continue managing my sin on my own, living like an orphan, and settling for cheap substitutes instead of the real thing.

This cycle is repeated, over and over, in my life as a Christian. As I am confronted with my sin, I can run to the cross, **repent**, and believe the gospel, or I can **resist** the cross and live like a spiritual orphan.

A Christian's position as a child of God doesn't change. All of us experience ups and downs in the cycle of faith. There will be times when my faith is strong, repentance is real, and I live more in the reality of who I am as His child. Then there will be times when my faith is weak, my heart not convinced that He loves me, and I will live as if I were a spiritual orphan.

Those who have not yet asked Christ to forgive their sins are doomed to spin around in the bottom circle, desperately seeking ways to manage their pain and brokenness. They crave acceptance and fulfillment but seek it in what the world has to offer instead of finding it in the grace and faith offered through the cross. (To learn more, see "Starting a New Life" at the end of this book.)

This diagram shows both the believer and the nonbeliever that the solution to our despair is the same: we both need to run to the cross and put our faith and trust in what Jesus has already done for us.

Recently a friend's Facebook status said, **"If the gospel is not the best news you have ever heard, then you have misunderstood the gospel."** I have no idea of the original source of this statement, but I love it! The gospel really does change everything! It changes my position in Christ, gives me a new identity, allows me to enjoy life as His child, gives me all the blessings and benefits of being in His family, and infuses me with a purpose for living that is greater than myself.

These next few pages will help you understand this process in a little more detail. I hope that as God makes the gospel even more real in your life, this diagram will give you a way to share what you are learning with others and that God will use it in your own life to shorten the gap between your head and your heart!

AWARENESS OF **SIN**

God always seems to get our attention. Whenever I think I'm doing fine handling life on my own, somehow, someway, He manages to show up and force me to deal with my sin. He's like a full-length mirror that follows us around from room to room. We can ignore it for a while, but eventually we are forced to take a close look and see every flaw and blemish—all the ways we don't measure up to His perfect standard, the law.

That mirror of God's holiness can take a couple of different forms. As my view of God expands, so will my awareness of sin. He will use multiple means to show me my sin. He will expose my unbelief through His **Word** (Romans 3:20), through the

Holy Spirit (John 16:8–9), and through the **community of faith** (Galatians 6:1).

But what is it we are actually seeing in this mirror? If you were to write a definition of sin, what would you say? When I was a teenager, I had a youth pastor who challenged us to go a whole day without sinning. I look back and now realize that he had a very small definition of sin. For him, sin was all about actions. His definition included a lot of "behavioral" words that communicated "not measuring up," "falling short," "disobedience," "rebelling against God," etc.

Sin is about more than just behavior. We sin because we are sinful.

We prefer thinking about sin in terms of behavior/performance/actions. It's easier that way. It allows me to do two things: I can focus on specific sins and "deal with them." Then when I have cleaned up that area of my life, I can move on and work on something else. It keeps things nice and tidy, not messy and overwhelming.

Second, if I focus on sin as only a set of behaviors, then it gives me a justified way of puffing myself up. I can usually turn around and find someone who is more messed up than I am. What a relief! Besides, if actions and performance are the only measure, then honestly, some days I do okay. You could follow me around and you would see me interacting with friends, spending time with my kids, taking care of my family, and serving others. If sin is just bad behavior, then some days I'm doin' mighty fine!

But sin is about more than just behavior. Our sinful behaviors flow out of sinners' hearts. We sin because we are sinful. The danger of focusing only on the external actions is that as long as we maintain a small view of sin, then we will believe in a small cross and a small Jesus. It's a convenient way to keep Him at arm's length.

The result of the fall is not only that we are separated from God, but that we are also corrupt—tainted through and through. Even our best efforts are still marred by sin.

Let's pretend I am offering you a piping hot, melt-in-your-mouth Ghirardelli chocolate brownie with added chocolate chips (yum!). There's just one catch. Right before I give it to you, I put a drop of cyanide on the corner. Just a drop. You know exactly where it is, so you can eat around it. Would you eat it? Probably not. For a large amount of money? Maybe. You might convince yourself that you could break off that corner and still be able to eat a portion of the brownie from the opposite side without being hurt by the cyanide.

That's kind of how we often view our sin. *It has just corrupted a piece of us; a corner of my heart, but not the whole thing.* If I am diligent enough I can, with surgical precision, remove the parts that are corrupted by sin while the rest remains unscathed. What an inaccurate view! This view of sin keeps it manageable. Not only can I compartmentalize it, but it allows me to compare myself with others—and gloat.

A better analogy would be this: imagine that deliciously thick brownie mixture before it gets poured into the pan.

While it is in the bowl, I add some cyanide, stir it in, and then bake the brownies. Would you eat them now? No way! The risk is simply too great. The batter has been completely corrupted by the cyanide, and it has worked its way into the entire brownie. Even with surgical precision, there would be no way to extract only the contaminated areas.

This is what we are up against in our battle with sin. Sin has infiltrated and corrupted every aspect of our hearts. There is no area that has escaped the damaging effects of the fall. We are completely tainted with sin. It's not just that a part of me is sinful, and so I sin. *I sin because I am sinful.* Sin is so much more than just behavior.

Romans 1 gives us a pretty detailed picture of just how deep the rabbit hole goes, and verses 28–32 (NIV-1984)point out how desperate we are outside of Christ:

> *Furthermore, just as they did not think it worthwhile to retain the knowledge of God, so God gave them over to a depraved mind, to do what ought not to be done. They have become filled with every kind of wickedness, evil, greed and depravity. They are full of envy, murder, strife, deceit and malice. They are gossips, slanderers, God-haters, insolent, arrogant and boastful; they invent ways of doing evil; they disobey their parents; they have no understanding, no fidelity, no love, no mercy. Although they know God's righteous decree that those who do such things deserve death, they not only continue to do these very things but also approve of those who practice them.*

Although any definition of sin would include a list of behaviors like those in this passage, sin goes much deeper than what we do. If we miss this, then we put ourselves on a path that will continually keep the beauty of the gospel of grace *just out of reach.*

Romans 14:23 gives us an even broader definition of sin: "Everything that does not come from faith is sin." This is a game changer. It challenges my definition of sin and expands it to include all of my unbelief. The reality is that *all* sin is rooted in unbelief. We are constantly bumping up against the wall of our unbelief and lack of trust in the gospel.

Our unbelief shows up everywhere, such as when I

- *listen to lies that say that I'm not lovable*
- *believe that a promotion will solve my problems*
- *turn to food, alcohol, prescription drugs, or pornography to numb my pain*
- *work harder to earn God's favor*
- *use excessive dieting and exercise to satisfy deeper cravings*
- *need others to "need me" in order to feel loved*
- *have to control people and circumstances*
- *can't say no for fear of letting others down*
- *am anxious*
- *am critical of others*
- *look in the mirror and hate what I see*
- *demand perfection from my children*
- *live for the approval of others*
- *beat myself up over my failure*

Our unbelief is ever-present, and so often we don't even realize it. It shows up in the choices we make, the idols we construct, and the perspectives we have on our circumstances. This brief list is just the beginning.

In the same way the gospel **changes** everything, our unbelief **corrupts** everything. I love how Paul David Tripp describes the beauty of being made aware of our sin and unbelief. He says, "Accurate self-assessment is the product of grace. It is only in the mirror of God's Word and with the sight-giving help of the Holy Spirit that we are able to see ourselves as we actually are."[2] Until we see ourselves clearly, we will never understand the sweet gift of grace we have been given.

DIGGING *Deeper*

At the end of each section you will find a few questions I hope will be helpful for you (and your group). Don't feel you have to discuss or answer every one, but I hope you will take the time to allow the Holy Spirit to cement these truths into your heart. For more information, see "Using This Book with a Group" near the back of the book.

1. What did you learn about sin and the gospel that was new to you?
2. Try to write an accurate definition of sin that includes more than just behavior.
3. What's the difference between viewing the gospel as *just* the "doorway" of your salvation versus. viewing it as *both* the "doorway" and the "pathway" of your salvation?
4. How have you made God small? How does having a small view of God relate to a small view of your sin? (and vice versa?)
5. God gets our attention through a variety of means. The three that follow were mentioned in this section. Can you think of times when He has used any of these in your life to make you aware of your sin?

- His **Word** (Romans 3:20)
- the **Holy Spirit** (John 16:8–9)
- the **community of faith** (Galatians 6:1; Matthew 18:15–20)

6. Just how deep does the rabbit hole go? The answer is sobering. Read and reflect on Romans 1:18–32 and Romans 3:9–20.

7. Take a moment to prayerfully reflect on the sinful attitudes and behaviors that trip you up on a regular basis. Perhaps you are a habitual worrier, or you often experience negative emotions like anxiety, envy, fear, or pride. List as many as you can—and not for the purpose of beating yourself up. Jesus loves you and has paid the price for these sins already. But knowing the pitfalls within your own heart will give you an advantage in learning a new way of repentance and belief.

2

REPENTANCE: A SWEET GIFT

As God exposes my unbelief and makes me aware of sin, I have a choice. One way to respond is to deal with my sin and failure through the gospel. I can remember how much He loves me and how He proved that on the cross. Then I can run to Him with a repentant heart, a heart that wants to receive what He has done for me. Repentance means, "I get it, God. I am sick over my sin the same way You are sick over my sin. I trust You to forgive me and remake me." The word *repentance* literally means "to turn around." In *The Wounded Heart*, Dan Allender describes it as a "profound internal shift in the perceived source of life."[1]

TRUE REPENTANCE

Repentance means abandoning myself to the grace of God. It means a full surrender to His love and care. It means I lean into grace while turning away from the things that have distracted my heart from Him. It means truly resting in His finished work on the cross.

Easier said than done.

As I write this I am really struggling.

How can I write about something I am not any good at? How can I describe something I am not really familiar with? How can I explain something I am just beginning to understand? (What I really want to do is find an exit ramp out of this chapter and just tell you to read the chapter on repentance in Dan Allender's book *The Wounded Heart*.)

Sometimes repentance is loud and messy; sometimes it is just a quiet letting go.

I don't know much about repentance. (Just ask my husband!)

But I know that repentance looks different from what we think it looks like. I used to think in order for my repentance to be real I had to be all weepy and emotional and that for other people's repentance to be real they needed to be down on their knees in front of me begging for mercy. Somehow I had a picture in my head of repentance that might have come straight from a cheesy scene in a "faith-based" film.

So, no formula here (sorry to disappoint you formula lovers!). Here are just a few observations.

Sometimes repentance is loud and messy, and sometimes it is just a quiet letting go. I remember one night in particular when God got my attention. David was out of town, and I was at the end of a long week of caring for our three kids by myself. At the time our younger son, Kyle, was around three years old, and we were muddling through the bedtime routine. (You would think with the third child we would have had it figured out. Nope.) He asked for a cup of water; when I brought it to him, he complained that the cup was the wrong color.

Too weary to fight, I dumped the water into a different cup and returned to his room. Let the games begin! He took one look in the cup and asked for more ice. I begrudgingly returned with more ice, and then he sweetly informed me that there was too much ice and now it was too cold. Time to start over. This continued for quite a while. When he was finally satisfied, I collapsed on my bed, and with clenched teeth I murmured, "I quit."

Immediately in my heart I heard a response: "You quit too late." At that moment I knew God was talking about more than that bedtime fiasco. He was showing me how independent and stubborn I am. How I cling to my plan until it absolutely doesn't work and **then** I cry out to Him. *It was clear. My problem is that I quit too late.* Always.

He is right. Repentance is an admission of how I live independently from Him. Repentance now meant that each day would start with a new phrase running through my head. "I quit, Lord; I can't do this without You." This was a huge turning point and a baby step in the direction of learning to live a life of dependence on Him.

That was years ago. My kids are almost grown, and Kyle is beginning his last year of high school. Time flies, but the issues in my heart are still the same.

This past year I began leading women's retreats, which I absolutely love. But I can be a bit of a control freak, so it is very hard for me to let go when I get involved in the planning process. At some point I am usually asked by the team if I have any suggestions for the songs to go with each session. I cannot tell you how tempting it is for me to respond quickly with a list of all the songs that tie in perfectly with each session, and which ones to begin and end with to create a "perfect package." I don't even need to pray about it. I already know what would work best.

But God made it abundantly clear that my response, other than letting them know the general content of each session, was to let them pick the songs. A few days before a conference in Atlanta, I changed one of my talks and knew that the hymn "Before the Throne of God Above" would be the perfect song to sing before or after the session. It was within forty-eight hours of the first session, and I had to literally *keep* myself from sending an email to the coordinator.

Staying out of the music selection is an act of repentance for me. Staying out of the music selection when I feel like I *really* have a good idea is an even bigger act of repentance for me. So you can imagine how I felt when I heard the first few strands of "Before the Throne of God Above" coming through the speakers to open the first session.

I guess that's why I love Allender's definition of *repentance*: "a profound internal shift in the perceived source of life." Because my "perceived source of life" will always be that which puts me in control and keeps me from leaning on God. For me, since being in control is my idol, repentance is typically going to involve letting go and leaning on Him. For someone else in that situation, repentance might have meant finding their voice and offering suggestions.

If your idol is the approval of others, then your repentance will be about recognizing that need, turning from it in a specific situation, and reminding yourself why you are already declared worthy by God. Another way of thinking about it is that repentance is turning from what you were looking at to give you life (approval of others) and looking instead to Christ and the approval He has already given you.

In some sense, repentance is going to look different for everyone, because each of us is clinging to something different. It's only when I turn from what I am relying on and shift my reliance back to Him that I really find the life and freedom that comes from repentance.

My favorite passage is Isaiah 30:15. I love it because it so accurately depicts my need for Christ, as well as my resistance to doing life His way. "In repentance and rest is your salvation; in quietness and trust is your strength, **but you would have none of it**" (emphasis added).

Repentance takes me to the root of my unbelief. It forces me to consider what I am trusting instead of Christ. So often I repent of the "fruit" of my sin—things like anger, pride, jealousy, and discontentment. I don't even consider the unbelief that has caused those sins to take root in my life—believing He doesn't love me, that He isn't in control, that He won't provide.

I will battle my unbelief daily! So daily repentance means I need to recognize when I am listening to those lies, confront the lie with the truth, and ask God to help me repent of the unbelief that led me to cling to the lie in the first place!

Repentance begins with conviction (that awareness of sin we talked about in the last section). Conviction will "look" different depending on how God is trying to get your attention. He might make you sick over your sin, or just restless and grumpy, but one way or the other, conviction sets in. Sometimes we think conviction or confession is repentance. But if saying, "I was wrong, and I am sorry" does not produce change, then it hasn't come from a repentant heart.

The goal of conviction and confession is to soften my heart and open up the door of repentance. Paul David Tripp describes it like this, **"It's only when I am grieved by my sin and acknowledge that this sin is heart deep that my confession will be followed by the turning of repentance."**[2]

The tricky thing is that repentance really is a work of the Spirit. It's a gift He gives us that restores our relationship with Him and brings healing. It's not something we produce as a way to manage our sin or fix ourselves. It's an internal shift, caused by the Holy Spirit, that sets us on a different path. It is a change that will show itself not only in a transformed heart, but in transformed attitudes, behaviors, and relationships. Repentance is a work of the Spirit; it's a gift He give us that restores our relationship with Him.

Somewhere along the way, we discover that repentance is not possible without surrender, without the "I quit." In the diagram, repentance is positioned as an upward turning that leads to restoration. But I know from experience that before you taste that restoration, it will feel like you are dying. It will smell like death. Because it is. Repentance is a dying to self, a letting go of what you are clinging to and admitting it isn't working. The uncurling of your fingers from trying to squeeze one more drop out of what you thought would bring you life is going to feel like it will undo you.

But it won't.

The goal of repentance is to remind me who God is and how much He loves me and to take me to the cross and straight into His arms. And that is where the party begins! That is what the Prodigal Son experienced when he returned home. And it's the same thing we can experience when we turn back to God. I am forgiven, and my relationship with God is restored. I am loved. That's why it says in Romans 2:4 that God's kindness leads us to repentance. It is a sweet gift!

FALSE REPENTANCE

False repentance: now, this, I am familiar with. This is what I know. I mean, really know. So often I would rather do anything than swallow my pride, confess my sin, and turn to Him in repentance. I would much rather ignore the gospel, bypass the cross, and resist the grace, love, and forgiveness of Christ. Basically, I reject what I am craving—His grace—and head off on my own.

> I see managing my sin as a challenge: How will I get out of this?

As I cruise away from the cross, I'm left with the question of how to deal with my sin and the conviction that weighs on me. I know I am broken inside. I know I'm bringing destruction into my life and the lives of others. I know my sin is "heart-deep." So what do I do?

I personally see managing my sin as a challenge: How will I get out of this? Through this? Around this? Other people respond in the opposite way—they crawl into a hole and beat themselves up. Either way, **it's amazing how much we can make managing our sin look like repentance.** Don't be fooled—it's absolutely not!

I'm an expert at this. I can even fool myself. I often think I am "dealing with my sin." After all, I feel bad; I'm really sorry a situation brought pain to people; I wish things were different, etc. But instead of fleeing to the cross and admitting my sin, I try to deal with the issues on my own—and usually in a way that makes me look good. This is false repentance.

Here are some of the common techniques I've used:

Blame-Shifting: My sin isn't as bad if I can show that someone/something else is the real problem. *If you knew what I've put up with for so long, you'd be angry too.*

Just "Fix It": My sin isn't so bad if I can figure out a way to prevent it in the future. *I've got a plan. Next time this happens, here is what I am going to do...*

Beating Myself Up (Contempt): I will really be taking sin seriously if I allow it to make me feel terrible. *I always make the same mistakes. I never get it right. I don't deserve to be loved.*

Minimizing: My sin won't be as bad if I can compare it to other things that are much worse. *Yelling one time after dinner is not that big of a deal compared to how badly the kids have behaved today.*

Denial: My sin isn't bad if it's not even sin. *Everyone struggles with this. It's just part of being human.*

Trying Harder: My sin will be manageable if I apply myself and work on the problem areas. *I'm going to learn to be more patient and not get uptight when things don't happen the way I want them to.*

Getting Defensive: (Does this really need an explanation?)

Do any of these sound familiar?

Imagine that one of the bathrooms in your home has gotten completely out of hand. No one has cleaned it in months. (Welcome to my world!) How could you respond?

- You might start by blaming other family members for the messes they have made.
- You could bravely jump in there armed with a bucket of Clorox and rubber gloves. (Scrubbing Bubbles has got nothing on you!)
- You might be tempted to sit on the floor and cry because you are such a failure and can't even manage to keep a bathroom clean.

- You could walk in, look around, pick up a towel off the floor, flush the toilet, spray everything with Lysol disinfectant and then walk out thinking, "I've seen worse."
- You could just put a big sign on the outside of the door that says, "Out of service until further notice!" and walk away.

When it comes to sin and our hearts, all of these are examples of false repentance. The crazy thing about the methods that we use to manage our sin is that they "look" a lot like repentance. But in reality all we are doing is managing our sin. And managing your sin is not the same thing as repentance. Unfortunately, the church is full of people who are great at managing their sin. But many have rarely tasted the sweet gift of repentance or the freedom it brings.

We are **totally incapable** of fixing our brokenness. A cheesy way to say it would be, "The only way out is to surrender and allow Jesus to 'clean the bathroom.'" Cheesy or not, the reality is He's the One who restores our hearts from the inside out. Relying on Him to change us is true repentance.

I love Isaiah 30:15 so much because it tells me the truth about myself. It tells me the source of my salvation and strength and explains how I refuse it. False repentance is a fake attempt at dealing with my sin. It's insidious and destructive. The scary thing is that it often "looks" like righteousness. But most of the time we don't realize it. While sometimes looking and feeling like true repentance, false repentance actually leads me further from the cross and away from Christ. False repentance is trying to solve our problem with sin with our own methods and means instead of relying on Jesus, which is exactly the image that is put before us in Isaiah 30:12–17. Verses 13 and 14 describe how devastating our sin is: "This sin will become for you like a high wall, cracked and bulging, that collapses suddenly, in an instant. It will break in pieces like pottery, shattered so mercilessly that among its pieces not a fragment will be found."

Wow. That's intense. It got my attention.

That description of sin is what makes verse 15 so glaring when it describes the gift of repentance and then claims, "But you would have none of it."

Why? We get the answer in the next two verses. We reject repentance because we have our own plan: "You said, 'No, we will flee on horses . . . We will ride off on swift horses'" (Isaiah 30:16). We have horses! Fast horses!

Giddyup!

Relying on our own plans seems so silly, right? But isn't it the way we respond? We cling to something else, thinking it will be what heals, rescues, saves, or satisfies. Often, we seem to be doing something proactive about our sin. In reality we are simply managing it, and that leaves us empty every time, like a broken cistern that can't hold water (Jeremiah 2:13).

False repentance is nothing new. Jesus encountered false repentance with the Pharisees and called them out in the strongest way possible: by cursing them.

> Woe to you, teachers of the law and Pharisees, you hypocrites! You are like whitewashed tombs, which look beautiful on the outside but on the inside are full of the bones of the dead and everything unclean. In the same way, on the outside you appear to people as righteous but on the inside you are full of hypocrisy and wickedness. (Matthew 23:27–28)

I can tell when I have fallen into the trap of false repentance. It feels like I am free-falling, relying on myself as the solution to my sin instead of the cross. I may start off feeling strong and powerful, but I end up feeling isolated, disconnected from God, and living like an orphan. I dig the hole deeper and deeper, working harder and harder to take care of myself, and finding myself more and more dependent on fulfilling my cravings and desires. This is a miserable place to be. And false repentance is the very thing that fuels our idolatry.

1. Did you learn anything about repentance that was new to you?

2. Luke 18 includes both parables and individual encounters with Jesus. We get a glimpse into the hearts of six types of people: a widow, a tax collector, a Pharisee, a group of children, a rich man, and a blind man. To which of these people can you relate? What do these exchanges teach you about humility, performance, and repentance?

3. Which type of false repentance do you typically rely on to manage your sin? (These are just a few. There are many more, trust me!)

    - **blame-shifting**
    - **fix-it**
    - **self-contempt**
    - **minimizing**
    - **denial**
    - **trying harder**
    - **getting defensive**

4. Do you remember a time when you experienced the gift of repentance? What led to this, and how did it feel? How did you see your repentance impact your feelings, actions, and relationships?

5. In your own words describe the difference between repentance and false repentance. What is the source for each?

3

RESTORATION of RELATIONSHIP

Before we can talk about restoration, we need to remember that even though repentance leads to restoration, renewed intimacy with God, and ultimately to joy, it is not going to feel intimate and joyful initially. That upward turn involves surrender, and repentance takes us to that place we desperately try to avoid—dying to ourselves. It's going to be hard.

RESTORATION

Ironically, it's often easier to take that downward turn away from the cross—away from relationship. Actually it just *feels* easier, maybe even life-giving, because it takes us back to the comforts of "home," the place where we have spent most of our time wallowing. (And it's where most of our friends are hanging out anyway!)

But restoration is what our hearts truly long for. And restoration is only possible because of what Jesus accomplished on the cross through His death and resurrection. The sin that separated me from God has been dealt its final blow on the cross. Jesus has given me a completely new life in Christ, and also a new identity. I am not the same.

Let's take a closer look at what restores our relationship with God. As Jesus hung on the cross, He took on the role of the sacrificial lamb in the Old Testament. He takes on our sin and the resulting separation from God for us. He endured the punishment I deserved. While He hung and bled, separated from His Father, God poured out His wrath on His only Son. God's anger burned against sin. But it also burned against *my* sin—my very real particular sins of anger, jealousy, gossip, a critical spirit, arrogance, insensitivity, idolatry, unbelief, and more. The rebellion that boils in my heart today was laid on Jesus, and He took the punishment I deserve.

He was judged guilty so we could be declared forgiven.

If God *poured out* His wrath, then it means **there is no more wrath left**. He is not angry with me anymore. **When I repent, He welcomes me home with open arms.** He throws a party (just like the father did for the Prodigal Son in the parable told in Luke 15). That's why just before Jesus died on the cross He was able to say, **"It is finished."** He had endured the punishment we deserved, and the debt of sin was paid in full.

Jesus endured the wrath of God *for us* so that we do not have to be punished for our sin. If the story ended there, it would be incredible. But it doesn't. In addition to paying for our sin, He also gives *us* His righteousness. **This transaction moves us from being objects of His wrath to being recipients of His grace.** It restores our relationship with God and gives us a new identity. God sees us differently now that we are given the righteousness of His Son.

> Like the rest, we were by nature deserving of wrath. But because of his great love for us, God, who is rich in mercy, made us alive with Christ even when we were dead in transgressions—it is by grace you have been saved. (Ephesians 2:3–5)

Imagine you owe a bank one billion dollars. (Now that's a shopping spree!) Think how it would feel if a friend came to you and told you, "The debt is paid." Then she opened an envelope from the bank and showed you an account statement that clearly indicated you owed nothing. That would be unbelievable, and you would feel an incredible burden lifted from your back.

But that still wouldn't mean that you have money to pay the mortgage or that you would not go into debt again in the future.

So imagine that same scenario with a slight twist. Your friend shows up with the account statement and tells you the debt is paid. But when she shows you the statement, instead of simply showing a balance of zero, the account shows a balance of one hundred billion dollars! Now that would be overwhelming! You would never have to worry about money again.

But your friend tells you it gets even better. Not only does the account have one hundred billion dollars in it today, but it will have one hundred billion dollars in it tomorrow. It will never change. No matter how much money you spend, every morning the balance in the account is one hundred billion dollars. It's like a billionaire's *Groundhog Day*!

That's what happened at the cross. It wasn't just that the debt of our sin was paid by Christ, but that we also received His **infinite righteousness**. When we were united with Him in His death, we were also united with Him in His resurrection. God looks at you and sees the righteousness of His Son—a righteousness that will never fade or "run out."

Consider these verses:

> God made him who had no sin to be sin for us, so that in him we might become the righteousness of God. (2 Corinthians 5:21)

> But God demonstrates his own love for us in this: While we were still sinners, Christ died for us. Since we have now been justified by his blood, how much more shall we be saved from God's wrath through him! (Romans 5:8–9)

> We have been made holy through the sacrifice of the body of Jesus Christ once for all. (Hebrews 10:10)

> He has reconciled you by Christ's physical body through death to present you holy in his sight, without blemish and free from accusation. (Colossians 1:22)

This transaction, where He takes my filthy rags and in exchange gives me His robe of righteousness, is what changes me. It changes our position before God and gives us a new identity as His children, clothed in His righteousness. **This is why the gospel changes everything!**

But it is easy to forget the basis for our salvation and relationship with God. That's why remembering is so important.

Restoration breeds hope, joy, and freedom. It's the promise that one day, in spite of my circumstances or my pain, God will make all things new. Sometimes when I read my Bible I write down in a little journal verses that stand out to me. One day I was skimming through Isaiah chapters 41–46 and wrote down this string of verses. They are in no particular order, and this is taken straight out of my journal.

> *Do not fear, I am with you. I have called you by name, you are mine. Remember these things, for you are my servant. I have made you. I will not forget you. I have swept away your offenses like a cloud, your sins like the morning mist. Return to me for I have redeemed you. I will lead you by ways you do not know, along unfamiliar paths. I will guide you. I will turn darkness into the light before you and make the rough places smooth. I will not forsake you. I will pour water on thirsty land and streams in the dry ground. I will pour my Spirit on your offspring and my blessings on your descendants. Forget the former things. Do not dwell on the past. See I am doing a new thing. I am making a way in the desert. Even to your old age and grey hairs I am he. I am he who will sustain you. I have made you, and I will carry you.*

I go back and read this often as a reminder to anchor my hope on the restoration and redeeming work of Christ. Because of the resurrection, **God will make all things new!** This gives me hope, especially on those days when I am either discouraged by my sin, overwhelmed by the pain swirling around those I love, or grieving over relationships that are not working. I long for the day when all of these things will be made right. I know it is coming!

ISOLATION

In the same way that repentance leads to restoration and intimacy with God, false repentance leads to separation, isolation, loneliness—and eventually idolatry.

> **We crave something to fill our emptiness.**

In our efforts to manage our sin, we are really striking out on our own and leaving God behind. When we do this we're rejecting both Christ's forgiveness and His righteousness. So we don't get to experience the **forgiveness** that comes from repentance ("There is now no condemnation for those who are in Christ Jesus," Romans 8:1), and we also don't receive the **righteousness** that comes through Christ ("God made him who had no sin to be sin for us, so that in him we might become the righteousness of God," 2 Corinthians 5:21).

We are left empty in all the ways that really matter. We respond to our **guilt** in the only way we can outside of Christ: by managing our own sin through false repentance. We respond to our **emptiness and lack** by trying to create our *own* righteousness through idolatry.

When Paul wrote about the Israelites' dedication to works and performance, he said, "Since they did not know the righteousness of God and sought to establish their own, they did not submit to God's righteousness" (Romans 10:3).

This is crazy talk! Did you catch that? They rejected the righteousness that Christ willingly gave them and settled for their own human-made righteousness. That's like stiff-arming God and saying, "No, I'm good. I got this." *Really?*

Several years ago one of my friends, Kelly, was a single mom juggling a career and two children on her own. (I wish you could hear her whole story–a beautiful one of brokenness and redemption.) During this time, her teenage daughter was really struggling with the rejection of her father and attached herself to a rough group of kids. She had run away before, but this particular time they had no idea where she was, and it had been several days. Here is an excerpt from the email she sent when her daughter finally came home:

> She is home. She was dirty, tired, hungry, angry, and belligerent but physically intact and arrived on her own

accord . . . or more accurately arrived by God's good mercy and on the breath of your prayers.

I don't know where she went or what happened while she was gone for four and a half days, and there is still no clarity on why she ran away. She is angry and wild-eyed. She said very little to me and I to her. She almost went into a fit of anger when I told her we were worried and we loved her.

While she showered I prepared a meal she typically likes. Although she was extremely hungry, she refused it and would only eat some pineapple out of a can. We have a feast of love for her but yet she is satisfied with the crumbs. She has rejected again any display of kindness or love. In the midst of this heart-wrenching experience, I have a moment of clarity. I can't help but see the parallel—my dearly beloved daughter, for God knows what reason, is refusing our love. I do the same with my heavenly Father in my own walk, if you can call it a walk—more like stumbling—with God. He prepares a feast for me, and I refuse to come to the table!

This story still touches me today, perhaps because I'm so much like her daughter. God has given me *everything* in Christ—His righteousness, His forgiveness, His grace, and His love—a feast of everything I am craving. It's a feast of everything I need, everything I have already been given. And

I have the nerve to saunter by, open a cabinet, grab a can of pineapple, and say, "No, thanks. I'm good."

But that is *exactly* what we do—all the time. Instead of clinging to the righteousness of Christ and the worth He gives us, we set off to establish our own worth. We find ways to make ourselves feel competent, successful, happy, distracted, and satisfied. Unfortunately, these efforts always fall short, and we are continually on the lookout for the next thing. When I reject what Christ offers, I have to turn to *something else* to stop the endless cravings.

It reminds me of when it's the middle of the day and I am on the hunt for some chocolate. Any will do. Honestly, I'm not that picky. Actually I take that back. I'd prefer a Reese's or M&Ms, but if we don't have those, I'm not ashamed to admit that I'll settle for the chocolate chips stored in a container in that useless cabinet over the microwave. I don't need to eat the whole bag, a handful is enough, and then I'm set—for a while.

An idol is any substitute for Christ. It's the handful of chocolate chips instead of the Godiva Pearls. It's something we *hope* will do for us what only Christ can do. Idols never fully satisfy. That's why John Calvin called our hearts "idol factories." It seems there is always another idol on the conveyor belt.

What do you run to? What do you crave? Probably not a can of pineapple or a handful of chocolate. **What makes you feel you have arrived when you get it right or full of despair when you get it wrong? What do you have to have**

in order to feel like you are *enough*? What do you run to for comfort when you find yourself sitting at the bottom of the diagram? That's a good place to start when thinking about your own idolatry.

Volumes have been written on this topic, and there are incredible books and Bible studies available to help you get an accurate picture of your heart and the form your particular idolatry takes. If this is your first encounter with the idea of idolatry, I really encourage you to dig deeper into some of those resources. I also want to remind you that this is a process, and sometimes not an easy one. We spend our whole lives trying to cover up what is really going on inside. So to peel back a layer—even one or two—can be a slow and painful process. Be patient with yourself and what the Spirit is trying to show you. You are not taking this journey alone. **This process is not easy.**

Here are some diagnostic questions to help you begin the process of discerning what your own idolatry looks like. One or two of these questions will probably resonate with you and help you uncover your idol.[1]

What is my greatest nightmare? What do I worry about the most?

When I go to bed, what is my consuming thought? When I wake up, what is my consuming thought?

When I feel isolated, lonely, or out of control, how do I comfort myself?

What, when I don't get it, causes the most conflict in my marriage and relationships?

Is there a theme to the conflict in my relationships that might give me a hint as to what my idol is?

What do I crave, that without it, I am miserable?

What do I consistently complete this sentence with? If only I had ____________________, I'd be happy.

Here's a peek inside my heart. When I go to bed at night I am typically thinking about one thing: *What did I get done today?*

If it's been a "good day," I will have been really productive and efficient and served and loved others well. If it's been a "bad day," I will have had lots of interruptions, accomplished nothing, and still have a long to-do list waiting for me in the morning. I will have snipped and snorted at others along the way.

Can you guess what I'm thinking about before my feet hit the floor in the morning? Brilliant. You got it on the first try. I'm thinking, *What do I need to do today?*

Do you see what this reveals about my idolatry? It revolves around work, performance, accomplishment. It exposes where I get my value from and what I cling to as the source of my strength. It shows me more about my heart than I really want to know. But it is the scary truth.

What consumes your thoughts before you go to bed and

when you first wake up in the morning can tell you a lot about your heart.

You know what else can tell you a lot about your heart and your idolatry? Your anger.

What makes you angry?

I get angry when I can't get things done. I get angry when constant interruptions keep me from staying on task. I get angry when other people (as in my husband and kids) don't help me get things done around the house. The White Witch in Narnia has nothing on me when I want to get something done and no one wants to help. I need other people to feed my idolatry and when they don't, I get angry. My anger reveals my idolatry.

Idolatry is based on lies—lies about many things, but mainly lies about God. Somehow I have latched on to the lie that I am only worthwhile when I am productive. At some level I believe God loves me more when I am busy. A deeper lie beneath that is that being productive makes me feel in control. I desperately need to be in control, because I believe He is not. Lies. They are all lies. These lies feed my idolatry and keep me away from God.

I love Isaiah 44. It is too long to insert here, but I would encourage you to read it. The prophet took aim at the whole system of idol worship and mocked a blacksmith who created idols. He went into detail about how the blacksmith crafted an idol—and emphasized that it came from the same piece of wood used to build a fire and bake bread.

> All who make idols are nothing, and the things they treasure are worthless. Those who would speak up for them are blind; they are ignorant, to their own shame.... **Such a person feeds on ashes; a deluded heart misleads him; he cannot save himself, or say, "Is not this thing in my right hand a lie?"** (Isaiah 44:9, 20, emphasis added).

Idol worship is based on believing lies. Lies about God—that He won't provide, or satisfy, or be faithful. Lies that He doesn't love me, He isn't good, or He doesn't care. I often recognize the idol in my heart and try to repent, but I don't go deep enough to see the sin beneath the sin. For example, I may repent of my idol of approval but not repent that I don't really believe God loves me—which is the lie that is causing this idol to grow in my heart in the first place.

The other sneaky thing about idolatry is that idols are often a corruption of desire. Idols take something that is meant to be good (like working hard, building an emotionally healthy family, serving others, taking care of your body, being creative) and corrupt those desires so that they become ultimate things.

As idols expand in our hearts, they demand to be fed and worshiped. Feeding our idols becomes a full-time job that moves our hearts further from the only One who can really satisfy—Jesus.

When our idols are exposed, our tendency is to respond

with false repentance. We try to manage our sin and run damage control from the fallout of our idol worship. We tend to work hard or try to "get better" to solve our problem.

Once again, the only real solution to our idolatry is a more intense look at Jesus and what He offers us instead. Elyse Fitzpatrick gently reminds us of the true solution to our idolatry. "Only the extravagant love shown us in the gospel has the power to draw us away from other loves. The beauty of His grace makes everything else seem listless by comparison."[2]

As you ask God to take the blinders off your eyes and give you a way of seeing the unbelief that lies beneath your idols, and as you take inventory of the damaging effects of your idol worship and ask God to give you a repentant heart, don't forget to run back to the cross and back into relationship. A relationship with the One who is calling out, "I love you, and I am enough for you!" Rejoice that Jesus has already given you *everything* you are craving and longing for. He has already done it. He satisfied your need and made up for what you lack. You no longer have to reach for the can of pineapple or hold on to that lie.

As you look at the bottom circle of this diagram, ask yourself, "What fuels my vicious cycle of living like an orphan, isolated and disconnected from God?"

The answer is *lies*. Living like an orphan begins by believing lies about our sin, and then lies about how to manage our sin, which lead to lies about what will fill and satisfy our hearts. These lies make us believe we can manage life without God.

In the book of Jonah, just before he is belched from the belly of a whale, Jonah knowingly proclaims, *"Those who cling to worthless idols forfeit the grace that could be theirs"* (Jonah 2:8 NIV-1984).

Do you know what scares me most about my idolatry? *Clinging to my idolatry takes me further from grace.* It makes me more reliant on myself and less reliant on Him.

1. Read Ephesians 1 and make a list of all the spiritual blessings you have received in Christ. Your list will give you a great start in expanding your definition of the gospel and your view of God.

2. How would it change you if you really believed that God poured out His wrath on Jesus? (And that means there is no more wrath left to pour on you!)

3. Based on the answers to the diagnostic questions on page 63–64, what might be the idols of your heart? As you name those idols, consider what lies you believe that have given room for these idols to grow.

4. How does clinging to your idol "prop up your righteousness"? How does it feed you? Soothe you?

5. In what ways is your idol a corruption of a God-given desire and longing? How does Christ meet that particular need instead?

6. Read Isaiah 44 and Jonah 2. What do these passages teach you about idolatry?

So much has been written on the issue of idolatry, but here are two of my favorite quotes for you to ponder:

"An idol is the thing you get your identity from and the thing you're turning to for your righteousness. It is anything more important to you than God, anything that absorbs your heart and imagination more than God, anything you see to give you what only God can give."[3]

"Mankind's root problem is not merely an external, behavioral problem—it is an internal problem of the heart. Paul believed that one of the primary reasons human hearts are not more transformed is because the affections of people's hearts have been captured by idols that grip them and steal their hearts' affection away from God (Ephesians 5:3–5). The reason why you commit a sin is because you don't believe God is first, and that He will provide for you."[4]

4

RENEWED IDENTITY: CHILD vs. ORPHAN

The insidious thing about sin and the human heart is that what we worship will eventually define us—and shape our identity. The cycle then continues, because who we are determines much of what we do. **It is crucial to understand our true identity—because eventually it will impact everything about us.**

Two of our children ran track in high school. One day after practice, their coach had the athletes do an interesting exercise. He asked them to list all of the roles they currently had to fulfill—like student, runner, athlete, etc. He then said, "In a few years, many of you will be doing very different things and have a whole set of new roles. If you get your identity from what you do, what happens when you aren't doing it anymore?"

It's a good question. So often we let our identity be shaped by our season of life and our circumstances, both of which are fleeting. Your identity is who you are, not what you do. It's what defines you. It determines your perspective on your circumstances, your choice of actions, and your view of the future. **Getting your identity right is absolutely crucial to really getting the gospel.**

LIVING as HIS **CHILD**

Consider what happened when people encountered God, as recorded in the Bible's narratives. We see all sorts of examples of radical transformation. Scripture is full of stories of people whose identities were completely changed by an encounter with God, such as

- Moses, from a rural shepherd to a challenger of kings
- Hannah, from a barren woman to the mother of a prophet
- David, from a shepherd boy to a slayer of giants
- the Samaritan woman, from an adulterer to a disciple

When *we* encounter God through repentance and restoration, we get a renewed sense of who we were made to be and who we are as children of God. We are given a new identity and transformed from

- ashamed to unashamed
- unforgiven to forgiven
- slave to free
- enemy to friend
- unknown to known
- broken to healed
- orphan to child
- unloved to loved

How crazy is this!? Paul describes it like this:

> When we were underage, we were in slavery under the elemental spiritual forces of the world. But when the set time had fully come, God sent his Son, born of a woman, born under the law, to redeem those under the law, that we might receive adoption to sonship. Because you are his sons, God sent the Spirit of his Son into our hearts, the Spirit who calls out, "Abba, Father." So you are no longer a slave, but God's child; and since you are his child, God has made you also an heir. (Galatians 4:3–7)

A few verses later Paul makes this incredible statement: "But now that you know God—or rather are known by God" (Galatians 4:9).

Known. By. God. Let that sink in for a minute. Our relationship is not so much characterized by the fact that we can know God, but that He knows us. That He longs to be in relationship with us—a relationship that would not be possible without the cross.

Through this transaction on the cross not only are we forgiven, declared righteous, and given every spiritual blessing in Christ (Ephesians 1), but we are also adopted into His family and given the full rights of an heir. **To be forgiven would have been amazing enough. But to become family? To be known by God? That is the icing on the cake!** That's why J. I. Packer calls our adoption "the apex of our salvation."[1]

Just this week I was listening to Christine Caine, from the nonprofit organization A21, which fights for the end of human trafficking. She shared how her parents sat her down one day to tell her she was adopted. She was thirty-three years old. I can't imagine how that could disrupt your world as well as your view of yourself, your family, and your identity. But what struck me most about her story is what she found on her birth certificate. Instead of her name, she was given a number, and in the description it read, "Unnamed."

But all that changed when she was adopted.

Every adoption story I have ever heard involves a story of loss and restoration. The same is true for us. The Scriptures brilliantly portray this in numerous places. But my favorites are in Ezekiel 16 and Romans 9.

Ezekiel 16 is an allegory of unfaithful Israel depicted by

the graphic story of a child who was abandoned at birth. "No one looked on you with pity or had compassion enough to do any of these things for you. Rather, you were thrown out into the open field, for on the day you were born you were despised" (16:5). Thank the Lord the story does not end there.

We rebel against God, and He rescues and redeems us anyway!

"Then I passed by and saw you kicking about in your blood, and as you lay there in your blood I said to you, 'Live!'" (16:6) Then God made a declaration: "I gave you my solemn oath and entered into a covenant with you, declares the Sovereign Lord, and you became mine" (16:8).

Mine! I love that, and the story doesn't end there! The next few verses describe the tender love and care God takes in raising this child and how she grows into a woman whose fame and beauty spread among the nations.

Here's the kicker in verse 15: "But you trusted in your beauty and used your fame to become a prostitute." The remainder of the chapter goes into the sordid details of her wanderings and how she turned the good gifts God had lavished on her into idols, which she worshiped. Then we finally get to the end of the chapter where it says, "So I will establish my covenant with you, and you will know that I am the Lord. Then, **when I make atonement for you, for all you have done, you will remember and be ashamed and never again open your mouth because of your humiliation**" (Ezekiel 16:62–63, emphasis added).

We use the beauty and gifts God gives to rebel against God, and He rescues and redeems us anyway!

In Romans 9 we find another picture of adoption and an amazing declaration. It's found at the end of a difficult chapter where Paul wrote about the sovereignty, judgment, and mercy of God. Strangely, it closes with this picture of rejection and redemption:

> "I will call them 'my people' who are not my people; and I will call her 'my loved one' who is not my loved one," and, "In the very place where it was said to them, 'You are not my people,' there they will be called 'children of the living God.'" (Romans 9:25–26)

Paul is referencing a passage from the Old Testament, Hosea 1:10. To understand the full significance of this for our identity, we need to briefly review Hosea's story.

God told Hosea to marry a harlot and then have children. Each child received a name that displayed God's displeasure and judgment with the people of Israel. Hosea's third child was named *Lo-Ammi*, which means "not my people." (I almost think I would prefer to go unnamed.) If this were the end of the story, it would be depressing. But it is really only just the beginning. In the story of Hosea we see a picture of God's relentless pursuit of us—in spite of our wanderings and unfaithfulness. At the end of the second chapter of Hosea, we find the hint of a great reversal and restoration that is yet to come. In the passage from Romans, Paul reminds us that it's already happened. We have been changed. God reverses that judgment on the people, and in Christ fulfills the promise that "they will be called sons of the living God" (Hosea 1:10).

This is the kind of love and grace we have been enveloped in. It is *amazing grace*! Because of Jesus, our relationship with our Father is restored so we can live as His children: "To all who did receive him, to those who **believed** in his name, he gave the right to become children of God" (John 1:12, emphasis added).

With God as our Father, we have been given a new identity in Christ. Your identity is directly tied to who He is and what He has done for you, not what you can accomplish. **There is nothing left to add; He has done it all.** Here's an equation that shows how our identity as a child flows from the character of God:

He is. I am. As His child, my identity is hidden in the eternal love and steadfastness of Christ. My identity is defined by who He is—*not* who I am. The following chart gives a few examples of how this works.

God is	Therefore I am
Redeemer	Redeemed
Protector	Safe
Ruler	Under His control
Comforter	Peaceful
Sustainer	Hopeful
The One Who Sees	Known
Provider	Cared for
Lover	Loved

Some of these characteristics are easier to understand than others.

He is love therefore I am loved.
He is forgiver, therefore I am forgiven.

But some of the examples in the chart may not seem true to our experience.

He is healer, therefore I am healed.
He is restorer, therefore I am restored.

For many people, their present reality screams just the opposite. They would say, "I am not healed. I haven't been restored."

Yet.

This process is not over. God began a work that He will finish when we are united with Him in heaven. So there is an aspect to our identity that has a "not yet" component to it.

So maybe we ought to tweak the verb tense.

He is healer, therefore I am being healed.
He is restorer, therefore I am being restored.

We get a taste of our new identity now, but we won't be fully transformed until the new heaven and the new earth!

My new identity as God's child results in a chain reaction that eventually changes everything about me: how I view myself, my sin, my circumstances, my pain, even my ministry and service. **This is why the gospel changes everything. Once it gets a hold of my heart, the trickle-down effect is endless:**

- I will have a personal ministry, but not out of my own strength or sense of duty. (No spiritual treadmill allowed here!) Instead I will serve out of a response to what He has done for me.

- I will continually see myself as both a saint (forgiven) and a sinner (in need of forgiveness), clothed in His righteousness but desperately in need of His grace.

- I will view grace as not only what saves me, but what sustains me. His grace begins and finishes the work in my heart.
- I will risk loving others without fear of rejection or hurt.
- I will be able to extend to others the grace He has extended to me. I will refuse to carry a critical spirit into my relationships.
- I will not demand my idol be fed. Instead I will see that my idolatry represents a deeper longing, and I will turn to Christ to meet that need and thank Him for being enough for me.
- I will forgive those who have hurt me. I can do this based on full understanding of how their sin against me will be paid for one way or the other–either they will trust in Christ for forgiveness or they will spend eternity separated from Him. Either way, I no longer have to extract payment from them.
- I will not be bitter about my circumstances. Instead I will view them as being sifted through the hands of a loving God. There is no Plan B. This is Plan A.
- I will not fret. God is in control. He is capable of caring for me even when I do not understand His ways.

- I will rest in His perfect love for me by not striving to earn His acceptance or the approval of others.

This list is just the beginning, but you can see how once the truth of the gospel seeps into your life it ___________ everything! (Thought you might have caught on by now.)

Understanding our identity matters. *A lot.* Until I see myself as God's child, I will never feel secure or be able to live the life He intended me to live. In fact, living out my faith hinges completely on who I am in Christ and what He has done for me. I have seen this in my own life. The gospel *has changed* me, *is changing* me, and *will change* me! Nowhere have I seen this more than in working through my pain.

A way of understanding how our identity shapes how we live is to expand the equation to include a third step:

He is __________; therefore I am ______________; therefore I can _________________.

He is forgiver; therefore I am forgiven; therefore I can forgive.

Years ago, I was really struggling with a deep hurt that was eating me up. The damage was showing up in every area of my life. As God began to restore my relationship with Him, I felt He was urging me to offer forgiveness to the person who had been the source of my pain. Eventually, I was able to express it in a letter like this:

> *I know the healing I have experienced is from God, for He is the one who initiates forgiveness by Christ's death and He is the one who can "restore the years the locusts have eaten." It is only*

because of God's forgiveness of me that I am even able to forgive you. My faith is in a strong and loving God. I know He will continue to heal me from the effects of your wrong actions. He is my Redeemer and the one who makes me whole. He has restored my soul. Regardless of how you respond, God has shown me the pathway of forgiveness, and it has led me straight to the foot of the cross, where I have found comfort in the arms of a loving God and balm to heal the wounds of my broken heart.

It is interesting to reread this after so many years and reflect on what God has done since. Even back then, when I was just beginning this journey of rediscovering the gospel, the source of my healing was anchored in who God is and what He has done for me. As the gospel of grace seeps into our hearts, not only does it restore our relationship with God, but it gives us a new identity. It puts our hope in the restoration that is yet to come and gives us the courage to walk through our pain, knowing that we are hidden and held—and knowing that one day He will make all things new and the transformation will be complete!

LIVING as an **ORPHAN**

Unfortunately, in this life I will never fully live in the reality of who I am as His child. I will always be tempted to go my own way and manage my sin on my own. It just somehow seems easier than repenting and resting in Christ. And there are times when, even though I crave it, I will refuse His grace. I will reject the love of a Father and the comfort of the cross, convincing myself that my resources for managing my sin are adequate and that my idolatry is really not that big a deal. When I do this, my life quickly becomes a shadow of what it was meant to be as I live out of self-reliance rather than God-reliance.

Reading the book *From Fear to Freedom* by Rose Marie Miller opened my eyes to how I was living as a spiritual orphan.

I picked it up at a conference where Jack and Rose Marie Miller were speaking on the Fatherhood of God. I couldn't really follow all that they were saying—because I had not really tasted grace or grasped the fullness of the gospel. But on the way out the door, I bought her book. Later that night, as I read through the pages, I felt I was not only reading my own story but getting a spiritual diagnosis of my heart. *Finally* I had an explanation for my daily reality!

Close your eyes for a minute and picture an orphan. You might imagine an abandoned child on the streets of New York City, a starving child roaming the streets of Calcutta, or a toddler trapped in a cage in an orphanage in Guatemala. Let your senses make this picture come alive. Imagine not only the sounds and smells, but how that child will develop emotionally and spiritually if she is never rescued.

Now imagine that child being adopted but refusing to sleep in a bed—or leaving the dinner table to go and look for food in the streets, or chaining herself to her bed in order to feel safe.

It's hard to imagine, I know. But spiritually, *this is us*. We go on living as orphans even though we have *already* been adopted and brought into a family.

After hearing how the gospel transformed Rose Marie from living like an orphan to living like a daughter, I had a much clearer picture of what that might look like in my own life, but I needed a chart to help me really get it. Consider this chart like an X-ray to expose the ways you might be living like a spiritual orphan.[2]

	When I Live as an Orphan	When I Live as God's Child
I am . . .	Fearful, independent, untrusting, hopeless, bitter, insecure, self-reliant, and trapped.	Hopeful, dependent, trusting, joyful, secure, confident, and content.
And I . . .	Gossip, shift blame onto others, am critical in spirit, collect on what I perceive as others' debts to me, complain, control, and respond defensively.	Give grace to others without judging them, accept responsibility for myself and my actions, forgive and accept others, being quick to pray and full of faith.
I see God as . . .	An absentee father, who just tolerates me and who judges and condemns me and keeps score of every wrong thing I do; a taker.	A strong Father, a trustworthy caretaker, a sovereign Deliverer and Provider, a Giver; loving, forgiving, and faithful.
I look at sin . . .	The way the Pharisees or moralists do, focusing only on external actions and deceiving myself about my sin nature; considering sin only an occasional problem.	Focusing on the attitudes of my heart, and know that I'm worse than I think I am, realizing that even my best self-efforts evidence a lack of faith.
I see myself as . . .	A fixer-upper—guilt-laden and unworthy, but self-reliant on my own moral will power; trapped by circumstances and worried by what others think of me.	A forgiven sinner, free, dependent, and loved; a saint.
I see grace as . . .	Not very valuable to receive or even necessary for daily living, but something to aid my own efforts to earn God's favor (because Christ is not enough).	Totally necessary for my salvation and ongoing growth; what I depend on daily.

The two columns really just display the symptoms of an identity crisis. When we live as orphans, we are rejecting the identity we have been given in Christ and are creating our own: one defined by our past, our pain, and our circumstances.

Our past includes our family situation (current family and family of origin), our accomplishments, what others have done to us, or what we have done to others (both good and bad).

Our pain encompasses how we have been hurt by others, by our circumstances, and by our own choices.

Our circumstances include the season of life we are in (single, married, fertile, infertile, widowed, divorced, stay-at-home mom, career mom, single parent, grandparent, empty nester, senior citizen) and our current life situation (going through a divorce, fighting cancer, rising to the top in a career, excelling as an athlete, starting a business, transitioning from working at home to working full-time).

Here's the equation that shows the grip these three things might have in your own life:

I was	Therefore I am
Controlled	Bitter
Abused	Angry
Successful	Proud
Neglected	Independent
Misled	Anxious
Sick	Over protective
Criticized	Critical

If you're like me, reading that list probably made you cringe.

I see myself in many of those descriptions. I allow myself to be consumed by the residual effects of my past, my pain, and my current situation. When my situation is going well, I'm confident and in control. When my situation becomes difficult or desperate, I quickly can become fearful, frustrated, and angry.

When I live as a spiritual orphan, everything is up to me. I think that I succeed or fail based solely on my own effort. I can remember a time, back when our children were young and I felt completely inadequate in my role as a wife and mother, that illustrates this orphan spirit perfectly.

Earlier in the day I had stripped the beds and put all the sheets in the washing machine. As we were putting the kids to bed that evening, I realized there were no sheets on the beds and quickly ran out to the garage to switch the load. This is no big deal, right? I needed to put other sheets on the bed, let the kids stay up later, or just camp out in the living room on sleeping bags.

Well, I must have been out in the garage for quite a while because David came out looking for me to see if everything was okay. I cannot imagine how he must have felt when he saw me sitting on the garage floor, knees curled to my chest, leaning against the washing machine, bawling. I'm sure he heard me muttering, "I am such a failure. What kind of mother can't keep clean sheets on the bed? What kind of loser can't remember to change the laundry? I don't deserve to be a wife *or* a mother!" Of course he gently reassured me that it really was no big deal, and I finally went inside.

As a spiritual orphan, I might serve others, but I'll do it out of a sense of duty rather than devotion.

Remembering that story brings all those emotions right back to the center of my chest. Obviously, I had reached the end of my rope. In my case, living like an orphan means that I feel great when I get it right and miserable when I don't.

I transfer this same reality to my relationship with God. On days when I perform well, I pat myself on the back and grab my Pharisee hat and parade around tooting my own horn. On days when I fail miserably, I put on sackcloth and ashes and beat myself up. Both results are completely dependent on my performance. It's all about me.

As a spiritual orphan, I might serve and minister to others, but I'll do it out of a sense of duty rather than devotion. I may remember that I'm justified (made right with God) by faith and the grace of Christ, but I'm pretty sure my sanctification (learning to live like Christ) is based on my self-effort. And so what God meant for blessing—living a life of dependence on Him, based on a heart of faith and worship—becomes a terrible curse, living on a treadmill of performance and disappointment.

There are two reasons you might be living like an orphan. In the first case, you might be a believer in Jesus but find yourself living more like an orphan than a child. This doesn't mean that you are not a Christian—*it just means that you are missing out on the most amazing blessings of our salvation.* You are not experiencing life as God intended, as an adopted child enjoying the benefits of being part of God's family.

Not long ago I went to Colorado to lead a retreat. The pastor's wife, who used to live here in Orlando, is a good friend of mine. Tricia sent me emails reminding me to drink lots of water before coming so that I wouldn't get altitude sickness. When she picked me up from the airport, there was a bottle of water in the car. When I went to bed, she gave me a glass of water. Throughout the weekend, she kept reminding me to drink!

Drinking water to avoid dehydration and altitude sickness is good advice. It helped me have a better experience while I was in Colorado. If I didn't drink water, I'm sure I wouldn't have died. It would not have been life-threatening.

But it would have ruined my weekend with an excruciating headache and the inability to hike and enjoy the beautiful mountains.

If you are a follower of Christ, then living your life in the bottom of this diagram does not mean that you are not a Christian. It just means you are missing out! It's like visiting Colorado and not being able to enjoy it because you weren't properly hydrated.

I needed to be reminded to drink water the whole time I was in Colorado. Tricia was great at that. And it's the same for us spiritually. We need to be reminded who we are and what Christ has done for us. Sometimes we need others to help us remember!

We need to remember the gospel, preach it to ourselves, repent, and run to the cross–back into relationship. **It's easy to forget what Christ has done, to think it's all about me, and to do it my way. The gospel compels us to think differently.**

The second reason you might be living as a spiritual orphan is *because you really are.* If you have never admitted your need for God, confessed your sinner's heart, and believed in what Christ did on the cross, then you are a spiritual orphan. You are living outside God's family, spinning around in the pit of orphan despair. But the answer for you is the same: Remember the gospel, repent of your sin, ask Christ to forgive you, and run to the cross. You'll be restored, invited into God's family, and given a new identity as God's child. (For more information about becoming part of God's family, see "Starting a New Life" at the end of this book.)

DIGGING *Deeper*

1. List as many people you can think of from the Old and New Testaments whose identities were changed by their encounter with the living God.

2. In the Gospel Eight diagram, the interior of the top circle reflects our identity in Christ. As you think about all the characteristics of God that can be squeezed in there, which ones are you the most thankful for?

3. Read Psalm 145. As you read, make a list of all the descriptions of God. As you look at each description on your list, see how who He is connects to your identity. He is ____________; I am ____________. Therefore I can ______________.

4. Which of the following do you tend to gain most of your identity from: your past, your pain, or your circumstances?

5. Look at the chart on page 87 comparing life as an orphan and life as a child. Circle all the words that best describe you. This is a good reality check but may be a bit sobering. Afterwards the typical response to this exercise is, "How do I move from living like an orphan to living like a child?" Based on what you have been learning, how would you answer that?

6. How would you re-create the "I was ___________; I am ___________" chart to reflect your own past and how it affects you in the present?

I was	Therefore I am

7. Read Ezekiel 16, an allegory about unfaithful Jerusalem. Although graphic, it is a perfect picture that shows how God rescues us as orphans and makes a covenant with us, His children.

8. What is your own story of *loss* and *restoration*?

5

RESPONDING to SIN

As His children we are given a new identity, and it begins to change everything about us. But it doesn't mean that we are perfect or that we are immune from suffering, struggle, or sin. The question then becomes, "How does who I am frame how I respond to these things?" Let's specifically look at how we respond to sin. When we are living like His children, our heart attitudes and outward actions will differ widely from when we are living like orphans.

A CHILD RESPONDS to SIN—THROUGH **REPENTANCE**

Even though I am a Christian, I'm still going to be confronted by my sin and unbelief and continuously made aware of my need for God. The beauty of the gospel is that the answer is simple for those who know they are God's children: *Remember who you are and run to the cross*: "In repentance and rest is your salvation; in quietness and trust is your strength" (Isaiah 30:15).

One of my favorite phrases in the Old Testament is "He remembers that we are dust" (Psalm 103:14). This knowledge of God's is such great comfort. He knows me, He gets me; and He knows that my faith is faltering. I believe, yet I don't believe. God knows exactly what to do with my unbelief.

Some of my favorite parts of the Gospel Eight diagram are the little arrows that show movement. To me, they speak volumes about how God's grace is always pursuing us. No matter where I find myself on this diagram, He is always inviting me back to the cross, back into relationship with Him. The cross is strong enough to bear the weight of all of my inadequacies, my fears, my pain, my sorrow, and my grief.

In the account in Mark 9, as Jesus, James, and John return from the transfiguration, a man has brought his sick child to the disciples for healing only to find that they can't heal him. When Jesus hears this, He exclaims: "You unbelieving generation.... Bring the boy to me" (v. 19). The father explains the son's illness and says, "If you can do anything, take pity on us and help us" (v. 22).

Jesus can't believe the question. "*If* I can? Of course I can! Anything is possible for one who believes" (Mark 9:23, paraphrased, emphasis mine). To that, the father exclaimed, **"I do believe; help me overcome my unbelief!"** Then Jesus healed his son (9:24–27).

I **love** this! *He remembers that we are dust. He gets me!* There are many days when I repeat it over and over in my head: "Lord, I believe. Help me in my unbelief!" The beautiful thing about this is that it is safe to confess our unbelief because He will not lash out at us. Remember, His wrath is finished!

There is a sweet group of moms who meet once a week at my son's school. We pray for the students and teachers, but we also pray for each other. Recently one of these dear women broke down and cried while she prayed, confessing her anger at the painful circumstances they were facing as a family, but also confessing her unbelief. As tears were streaming down her face, she prayed, "I am going to keep saying, 'I trust You, Lord,' until I start to believe it."

Like this friend, even with wavering faith, I can confess my unbelief and run to the cross, resting in my Father's love and what Christ has done for me.

Isaiah 30:15 describes how He offers us repentance and rest, but we refuse. A few verses later (Isaiah 30:18; incidentally this is directly after the boasting about those fast horses, remember?), we get a beautiful picture of God's longing for us, even though we may resist Him: "Yet the Lord longs to be gracious to you; therefore he will rise up to show you compassion." Even though we prefer our plan of fleeing on horses to trusting Him, He still *longs* to be gracious to us. He *wants* to show me compassion. No matter where I am, or how far I have wandered, He wants to love me. And to get that love, I don't have to do *anything*! That blows me away.

How can we get a grip on how much we are loved in spite of how our sin and unbelief continues to wreak havoc in our hearts? That's why getting this identity piece about who we are in Christ is so essential! When we really understand our identity in Christ, we will realize that there are three things that are true about us—**all the time**.

1. Because I am forgiven and clothed in the righteousness of Christ, I am seen as a saint in His eyes. I am secure. Nothing I do can change that.

2. Because I am a sinner, corrupted by a sinful nature, I will continue to sin.

3. Because I am His child, He will continually pursue me by His grace and draw me back to Him.

Saint. Sinner. Child. Say those three times fast. These are equally true all the time. Any one does not negate the others. If we only grasp the part that we are sinners, then we will be characterized by self-loathing and moaning and groaning about our unworthiness. The focus stays on us and not on Christ. Focusing solely on our sin minimizes what Christ has done. On the other hand, if we focus only on the fact that we are saints—those who are made holy by God—then we tend to minimize our sin, which makes a mockery of His death. If we forget that we are His children, we will miss out on the beauty of the relationship and the fact that we are known by God. Seeing myself as **both** a saint and a sinner reminds me **I am desperately in need of His grace—it is what saves me and it is what propels me forward in my growth as His child.**

Three things are true about me all the time: I am a saint, a sinner, and His child.

I love the way Elyse Fitzpatrick captures the essence of our relationship with God—and the very reason we don't need to fear repentance. In her speaking and writing, Elyse constantly reminds us that we are both "welcomed and loved." To me, that phrase invites me into relationship and into repentance because I have nothing to fear. There truly is no more condemnation.

AN ORPHAN RESPONDS to SIN—THROUGH **SELF-RELIANCE**

When living like an orphan, I will at times look deep into the mirror and feel the stirring of the Spirit prompting me to repent and believe. Turn and trust. It's easy to say but hard to do.

Remember the "But you would have none of it" phrase from Isaiah 30:15. So often I choose to bypass the cross, striving to find my own way out of the pit so I can escape on horseback! Ironically, this self-effort simply drives me deeper into a life of self-reliance that takes me further from God.

I reject the simple (but hard) way of the gospel (repent and believe) and choose a more difficult path of managing my sin and feeding my idols—a journey that requires me to summon my energy, work hard to gain the approval of others and God, and either bury or nurse my pain. Here I go, circling around and around and around.

This is what happens when we make repentance primarily about fixing our own behavior and "getting better." Just this week I saw a tweet by speaker and writer Kendra Fletcher that said, "The answer isn't to suck it up, sacrifice for others, homeschool your kids, control your anger, or avoid spaghetti straps. The answer is Jesus." Kendra gets it: The point is not our best efforts. The point is God's grace.

The problem with trying to "get better" is that we start with the fruit instead of the root: try harder, do more, pray more, have a quiet time, do this list of ten things that lead to holiness, and on and on. It's not that our actions are unimportant; it's that our actions can't be the first thing we focus on. Otherwise, we end up like the Israelites.

> The Gentiles, who did not pursue righteousness, have obtained it, a righteousness that is by faith; but the people of Israel, who pursued the law as the way of righteousness, have not attained their goal. Why not? **Because they pursued it not by faith but as if it were by works.** They stumbled over the stumbling stone. (Romans 9:30–32, emphasis added).

The Israelites stumbled over Christ because they couldn't accept that their righteousness was not based on their *own effort.* Is there any chance we, too, might sometimes fall into thinking that our righteousness is based on self-effort?

In Galatians, Paul expresses how easily we get confused in our understanding of *why* God works in us. He says,

> Are you so foolish? After beginning by means of the Spirit, **are you now trying to finish by means of the flesh?** . . . Does God give you His Spirit and work miracles among you by the works of the law, or by your ***believing what you heard***? (Galatians 3:3–5, emphasis mine).

Believing what you heard=faith. That's where our transformation begins. With faith.

At the end of the last chapter, you responded to the Orphan or Child chart by considering how we move from living as orphans to living as children of God. Most of us look at those two columns and know where we *want* to be. But too often we associate change with works (what we accomplish). God transforming us to live as His children is a work done through His Spirit by faith. The answer to how we move from living like an orphan to living like a child is to *believe what we heard.* Or in another words, *faith*! It is as easy and as hard as the challenge of Jesus: to repent and believe.

What types of things do I need to believe to see real change take place? I need to remember and believe the truth about

- who Christ is
- what He has done for me
- who God is

- all the spiritual blessings I have in Christ
- God's Word
- God being in sovereign control
- God's love for me
- God's knowledge of me
- God's awareness of me
- God's delight in me
- and on and on and on . . .

One day years ago I was really struggling and called my friend Tricia and unloaded on her. I was pretty much a wreck, so she invited me over for lunch. As we sat and talked, Tricia made a statement that has stuck with me and become a part of my spiritual DNA. She said, **"The truth can transform you as much as a lie can destroy you."** So simple, but profound.

The statement launched a whole new journey in my heart to help me uncover the lies I believed and how they were strangling me. No matter what emotional hole you are sitting in, you probably got there by believing lies. God can rescue you from the pit when you turn your eyes and heart back to Him.

Believing the truth is a fight. Your mind and heart conjure up so many lies about God, yourself, your pain, and your circumstances. Satan is the father of lies, and he wants you to be suspicious of God's love and plans for you. When living in the vortex of life as an orphan, you will have to fight a battle to tell yourself the truth when the lies are screaming louder. Even as I write this, I am battling the lies and voices in my head. Honestly, sometimes the insecurities make me feel like I am back in middle school. *Who do you think you are? What do you have to say that hasn't already been said? God only uses people who have their act together. If these readers knew what a mess you are, they wouldn't even read this. Blah, blah, blah.* **Only truth can silence the lies.**

In Rose Marie Miller's book *From Fear to Freedom*, she uses an illustration to describe our desperation. When we are stuck living as orphans, we are like a caterpillar encircled by a raging inferno. There's no way a caterpillar can escape a ring of fire. Deliverance can only come if a hand reaches down and pulls it out of the fire. *Deliverance comes from above.*[1]

> I waited patiently for the Lord; he turned to me and heard my cry. He lifted me out of the slimy pit, out of the mud and mire; he set my feet on a rock and gave me a firm place to stand. He put a new song in my mouth, a hymn of praise to our God. Many will see and fear the Lord and put their trust in him. (Psalm 40:1–3)

For us, being rescued out of our orphan pit is both as **easy** and as **hard** as *remembering the gospel.* On one hand, it's simple just to admit my sin, ask God to forgive me, then enjoy a restored relationship with Him. On the other hand, fighting the lies, swallowing my pride, admitting my need, confessing my sin, abandoning my idols, refusing to be defined by my pain—these can be the hardest things ever!

Most of the time I can't even tell when I am living like

an orphan. I am so blind. A few months ago, David and I were having one of those "discussions" that was not getting resolved. It was making me grumpy, irritable, and angry. My friend Valerie and I exercise together a few times a week, so she had been listening to me process it all for a few days. Finally, one day as I was putting my bike up into the garage and closing the door, she called out to me, "Ruthie, you know you are living like an orphan, right?" So I reached up and pushed the button to close the garage door. As I did, she jumped in the path of the detectors to stop the door from closing and boldly proclaimed, "And I'm not going anywhere until you admit it."

That, my friends, is good stuff! When we can't see it ourselves, usually our friends can. God puts them in our lives to help us remember the gospel and drive us back to Him and give us a taste of grace. We need people in our lives who can remind us to turn and trust, to lean in and depend on the One who is inviting us into relationship with Him.

DIGGING *Deeper*

1. When you turn and trust God, how do you view God's response to you? Is it filled with love, forgiveness, contempt, or disapproval? Read Luke 15, where Jesus tells three parables that give us a hint about how God responds to a repentant heart. What do these parables teach us about the heart of God toward us?

2. Based on this passage, how does your picture of God need to be adjusted to align with Scripture?

3. Why do you choose to manage your sin through false repentance rather than running to the cross for complete healing and grace? What is it that drives you to resist His grace rather than run to it?

4. What are the voices you hear in your head when you know you have failed or when you are afraid to fail? The messages you hear in those moments are a clue to the lies you believe. (Remember my story about forgetting the sheets in the washer in the previous chapter? What was I telling myself? What was I *really* believing?)

5. When you reflect on the pain of your past and the bitter fruit it has produced in your life, can you identify any vows you may have made that reinforce the lies you believe or are susceptible

to? Examples might be, "I will never let anyone see me cry," or "I can't count on anyone but myself." You may want to keep a record of these messages as the Lord reveals them. You must identify these lies if you want to sever their roots and begin to believe the truth.

6

REST or RESIST

You are probably familiar with the verse that tells how God says, "Be still, and know that I am God" (Psalm 46:10). This is a sweet invitation from a loving Father for us to rest, listen, and wait on Him. Yet I hate this verse. I don't do "still" very well, and I certainly don't do "rest" very well.

The intersection of the diagram where the two circles come together, asks the question, "Will I rest in or resist the gospel?" This reminds me of a railroad crossing sign, and as I battle my unbelief I can hear those warning bells a ringin'!

What happens at the intersection? Here's the short answer: *When the Spirit works in our hearts to show us our sin and point us to*

Christ, we can either run to the cross and rest in our Father's love and forgiveness, or we can resist the cross and make our own way, relying on our self-sufficiency and cheap substitutes for a Savior.

Now if you're like me, a longer answer will probably be a little more helpful.

> I feel more secure when I am micro-managing my world.

What does it look like to rest—a *rest* that leads to *rest*oration? Honestly, I am not sure I can give you a good answer. It is just so hard. For a long time I equated rest with inactivity, with not doing anything. That hardly seems to be the solution, for obvious reasons. But I am finding that a better definition might be "to cease striving." Striving is what makes me weary. Trying to earn my way, earn His love, earn others' approval. Striving eventually feels like a noose around my neck and leads to bondage, not freedom.

I choose striving over resting because I don't trust.

And the reason I don't trust is that I don't believe He loves me. And the reason I don't believe He loves me is that my experience seems to tell me otherwise. I often don't get what I want, and the sad reality is I let my experience and what I think is true trump the reality of what God says about me, my circumstances, and Himself.

The reason I don't rest in His love for me is that I am suspicious of His love. Letting Him love me and be in control of things puts me in a vulnerable place. I feel more secure when I am in control and micromanaging my world than when He is in control. *Do you hear the irony in that?* It reminds me of the daughter who chose the can of pineapple instead of a feast in Kelly's story. "No God, I'm good. I got this."

So what would it take to move me from **resisting** to **resting**? It comes back to repentance and faith: repenting of the lies I am believing that keep me from resting in Him and *replacing those lies with the truth. Turn and trust.*

I know that each of us struggles with a different set of lies. But in my life, these lies about God are the ones that sink me:

He isn't in control.

He doesn't know me.

He has abandoned me.

He doesn't act for my good (*my* definition of good).

He doesn't love me.

In essence, we have exchanged what is true about God for a lie. It is these lies that keep us from resting in Him.

TRUTHS THAT **TRANSFORM**

When I was a little girl my family lived overseas, and I always looked forward to someone sending us the J. C. Penney catalog. My favorite section was the bedrooms. You know those rooms with the matching curtains, rugs, wallpaper, and comforter, all in a print similar to one you would find on the outside of a box of tissues?

My eyes were always drawn to the canopy beds. I dreamed of sleeping under a canopy bed. It didn't help that we lived in Europe, and every castle and palace I visited had amazing canopy beds!

Since a canopy bed is so inviting, let's use that as an illustration to help us understand what it means to rest in the

Father's love. With four posts, we'll let each post represent a truth we need to believe about God in order to move from resisting to resting. Listed below is each truth and a few related verses that will help you understand each one.

God Is in Control

Acts 17:26; Psalm 139:14–16; Philippians 2:12–13; Psalm 115:3; and Psalm 33

This is a hard one to swallow isn't it? Mainly because it brings up so many questions. In a sense, we will never completely understand this truth and are going to have to live with the tension it brings. But it is essential for all of us to wrestle this one to the ground if we are going to live with a renewed perspective.

God Knows Me

Genesis 16; Psalm 103:14; Psalm 139; and Isaiah 49:15–17

He is intimately acquainted with my ways, sees me from afar, knows my name, and knows my heart. Both the story of Hagar in the wilderness and Jesus' conversation with the woman at the well give us just a sweet glimpse of how well we are known and loved! He is El Roi—the God who sees me!

God Will Never Leave Me

Joshua 1:5; Deuteronomy 31:8; Hebrews 13:5–7; and John 14:18–27

Not only does He know us, but He promises to always be with us. Even when accused of forsaking His children, He graciously responds by saying "I will not forget you! See, I have engraved you on the palms of my hands; your walls are ever before me" (Isaiah 49:14–16).

God Acts for My Good and for His Glory

Philippians 2:12–14; Romans 8:28–29; 1 Peter 1:7; Ephesians 1:11–12; Jeremiah 29:11; and Isaiah 55:9–11

This is another tricky one because of how we define the word *good*. Typically, we define *good* by what makes us feel happy, cared for, blessed, etc. But God's definition of our good is a wee bit different. He defines our good by what will bring Him glory. Ouch. That difference just might be a game changer.

These four truths alone aren't enough to make me want to rest. In fact, you would be a fool to fall back in that four-poster bed and rest based on those alone. Unless we become absolutely convinced that He loves us, then it's not worth the risk. Without His love binding these other four truths together, God is simply a controlling creeper, stalker, narcissist I should keep away from. If He doesn't love me, I don't want Him to be in control. If He doesn't love me, I certainly don't want Him to really know me. If He doesn't love me, I definitely don't want Him sticking around!

Many of us have had people who loved us but then hurt us. That can make it hard to trust that God will be good with His love.

So the fifth truth that ***God Loves Me*** is like the canopy covering that four-poster bed. I would say this is the most important truth of all—it makes the other truths comforting instead of creepy.

It reminds me of the song "His Banner over Me Is Love" that I used to sing when I was a little girl. It says, "I am my beloved's, and my beloved is mine" (Song of Solomon 6:3). It reminds me of Zephaniah 3:17, where it says, "He will take great delight in you . . . [he] will rejoice over you with singing."

It's this kind of love that gives me the security to take the plunge into that big canopy bed and rest! It's the only thing compelling enough to make me want to trust Him.

Many of us find letting God love us is difficult, even painful. **We don't trust Him to be good with His love.** The pain of our past keeps us from allowing God, or anyone, to love us. We end up letting our experiences trump what God says is true about Himself.

Yet my ability to rest in Him is directly tied to who He is. **Do I believe it or not? Am I willing to trust Him? Am I willing to let Him love me? Am I willing to believe He can heal and redeem the broken pieces of my heart? Am I willing to trust that He will be good with His love?**

These five truths are based on who God is—on His identity and His character. They can all be written in the top portion of the circle (along with about a zillion other truths about God!). Remember the five truths: *God is in control, God knows me, God will never leave me, God acts for my good and His glory,* and—overarching them all, *God loves me.*

If I asked you if you believed them, you would likely say yes. Not so fast.

It's hard work to uncover what we *really* believe about God, mainly because most of us have spent many years suppressing what we really think and feel about Him. **We feel anger, betrayal, and jealousy; yet we don't see how often these are rooted in a lie we are holding on to about God.**

Many years ago, in preparing for a talk, I collected a series of candid statements written to God from friends. Here are just a few:

I desperately cry out for friends who really know me and love me, and You leave me alone and disconnected. You don't want what's best for me.

God, why are You willing to sit back and allow "our" daughter to ruin her life with all these bad choices? Why are You not doing anything?! Are You really the "Father to the fatherless"?

Father, why have You delayed or denied a husband for me? Am I too broken—too ugly—or have my sins been so great that I blew it?

You've blessed all these other women with children but not me. You don't care about me or my desires.

I still feel guilty after all this time. You didn't forgive me.

I prayed for You to heal my mother. You didn't. She died. You are not a healer.

My husband has a pornography addiction. You are not powerful enough to break this cycle and save our marriage.

My husband left me for another woman. You could have stopped him, but You didn't. Where were You?

Every day for a year, I've begun my day fearful that I am a bad mother. You can't give me victory over my anxiety.

My cousin molested me throughout my childhood. You saw it all and didn't intervene. You must not be able to protect Your children from harm.

You asked me to share my heart with my small group. All I got was the blank stares. You set me up for rejection.

My thirteen-year-old daughter doesn't have a single Christian friend to encourage and support her, despite many efforts from us both. You've thrown her to the wolves!

It takes all the strength I have to get out of bed every day. You promised me "an abundant life," but all I have is depression. You lied.

Wow. Those are painfully honest confessions. Can we be that honest? Are you able to express how you really feel about God and your circumstances?

Does reading these heartfelt statements help you see how our perspective on our circumstances can expose what we *really* believe about God?

This is so important because eventually what we believe about God will show up in how we live our lives, walk through our pain, and make choices about the future. What we believe about God will show up in how we live our lives.

I don't really care what you ***say*** you believe about God. I care what you ***really*** believe about God. And what you really believe about God has a way of leaking out, eventually.

If the lies seem hidden from you right now, stop and ask God to begin a process of peeling back the layers and showing you what's really there.

What we believe about God will show up in how we live our lives.

You cannot begin the process of replacing the lie with truth until you first know what lie you are believing. I love the moment of clarity in the passage from Isaiah 44 we looked at earlier: "Is not this thing in my right hand a lie?" (v. 20).

It's amazing how often we hold on to lies with a fierce, white-knuckled grip. The Old Testament tells us of a woman who understood exactly what we are up against in this fight for faith.

The widow of Zarephath just might be one of my favorite ladies found in the Bible. We find her story in 1 Kings 17. I hope you will take time to read about this woman in great pain. She is a widow raising her son in a land shriveled by drought. She is at the end of herself, her hope, and her food. In fact, she is collecting wood to cook her last meal. If there was ever a woman stuck like a caterpillar in a ring of fire, she is it!

Along comes Elijah, prophet of God, who has been stuck

in a dried-up ravine being fed by ravens. (I am sure he smelled lovely!) He sees her gathering wood and asks her to make him a small loaf of bread.

I wish this were on YouTube. I would love to see the expression on her face or find out if she whacked him over the head with a stick. *Are you serious?* She has enough oil and flour for one more loaf of bread, and Elijah wants the little bit she has left for himself? She protests and lets him know just how desperate things are. But he sees right through her rant, directly into her heart, and says three words: *Don't be afraid.* Then he promises her that if she makes him a small loaf of bread, she will have enough oil and flour to make some for herself and that it won't run dry—ever.

For a woman in survival mode, this is the ultimate test! Will she give in to her fear? Will she listen? Trust? Or walk away?

We are just like the widow of Z! We are desperately clinging to our oil and flour, believing that what we **can see** is safer than what we **can't see**.

The widow of Z is a courageous woman. I want to be just like her when I grow up. She baked him some bread! And another loaf, and another, and another. (I would love to know what she was muttering under her breath when she made that first loaf!) The oil and flour did not run dry. There was always enough.

The widow of Zarephath trusted and was not disappointed. She opened the door for God to do a *new* thing in her heart. But it doesn't stop there. The end of the chapter records the account of her son getting sick and dying. This does not go over well, and in her anger she lashes out at Elijah and his God. Even though her wrath is directed at God and Elijah, her son is miraculously healed. By setting aside what she was clinging to (her oil and flour) and putting her trust and hope in a promise, she experienced the blessing of faith and repentance. She is rescued and boldly proclaims, "Now I know who you are and what you say is truth" (1 Kings 17:24). I love the irony. She is not even a Jew, and she is making a confession that the people of Israel had failed to make because they turned their backs on God and went their own way.

That's my prayer for all of us: that we can set aside what we are clinging to and say with the Widow of Z, **"Now I know who you are and what you say is truth."**

Then, and only then, can we fall back into that big canopy bed and rest. *Whoosh!*

DIGGING *Deeper*

1. Of the five truths in this section, which is the hardest for you to believe and why?
    - **God is in control.**
    - **God knows me.**
    - **God will never leave me.**
    - **God acts for my good and for His glory.**
    - **He loves me.**
2. Why is *really* believing God loves you essential to resting in Him?
3. The grid on the following page can be helpful in discovering the lies you are clinging to that keep you from resting in Him. Begin by writing **one** of the five truths about God, then answer the questions in each column. Work your way down. Begin with column A and then do column B. There probably will be multiple examples in each box. If you are doing this with a group, write down every example so you will begin to see how there is no area of our life that is not impacted by the lies we believe about God. As you work through this, it will reveal what you really believe about God and how it is impacting your life.

Pay special attention to the last two questions in each column and see how they are connected. Our idolatry emerges because of the lies we believe about God. For example, if we don't believe God loves us, we might end up idolizing people and needing their approval. In the second column the last question is, "What would repentance look like for me?" You can't answer that unless you answered the last question in column A, "What idol do I run to?" For example, if your idol is the approval of others, then your repentance might be about recognizing that need, turning from it in a specific situation, and reminding yourself why you are already declared worthy by God.

4. Read 1 Kings 17 and review the story of the widow of Z. How does her courage inspire you? What would you have done if you were in her shoes?

THE TRUTH CHART

God says He is ______________________	
I don't believe this truth because...	
When I don't believe this truth...	***If I really believed this truth...***
how do I relate to others?	how would I relate to others?
how do I view my circumstances?	how would I view my circumstances?
how do I view myself?	how would I view myself?
how do I relate to God?	how would I relate to God?
what idol do I run to?	what would repentance look like?

Note: For additional copies of the Truth chart, visit www.CravingGrace.org.

Here's a sample, filled in with the starting point of the attribute of God that He is Loving

God says He is Loving	
I don't believe this truth because... I don't feel like He loves me My experience tells me otherwise Bad things happen	
When I don't believe this truth...	*If I really believed this truth...*
how do I relate to others? earn their love want approval demanding hide manipulate	how would I relate to others? less demanding more gracious/patient willing to risk loving be real
how do I view my circumstances? as punishment up to me unfair frustrating hopeless	how would I view my circumstances? gift opportunity as discipline hopeful
how do I view myself? unloveable must work hard insecure - unknown afraid to love no confidence	how would I view myself? lovable safe fully known accepted secure confident cared for
how do I relate to God? distant earn love angry at Him suspicious fearful hide run away	how would I relate to God? open to Him trusting would let Him love me connected eager to run to Him
what idol do I run to? approval of others performance work control	what would repentance look like? not seeking others' approval resting trusting cease striving

Where
am I?

7

REAL LIFE and the CYCLE of GRACE

You've probably noticed by now that this diagram is drawn as a fluid figure eight.

Sanctification is a process, a process of becoming more like Christ—a process of recognizing *how great my sin is, how big the cross is, and how much I need* Jesus. It's a process of expanding my view of the greatness of God and becoming more dependent on Him and less self-reliant. It is a process of learning that my life is about making much of Jesus and not much of me.

I didn't always believe this. In fact, when I was twenty-one, if you had asked me to describe a "godly woman," I would have described an old lady with blue-gray hair who had "gotten it together" to the point she rarely needed Jesus' help. I may not have said it aloud, but I can *guarantee* you that is what I really thought deep inside. And I was on a mission to get there—before you! The glorious reality is that I am not going to "get better" unless my definition of "getting better" is needing Jesus more. As I see just how deep the rabbit hole goes, I will see more and more how desperately I need a Savior.

A humorous way for me to see how grace has captured my heart is to take a look back and remember what I would consider to be my "theme songs" while growing up. If you had been around me during some key stages of my life, what would you have heard me singing?

You would have heard me, as a preteen with a hairbrush "microphone" behind closed doors, belting Helen Reddy's "I Am Woman, Hear Me Roar." If you'd caught me as a senior in high school reeling from a series of destructive relationships, you would have heard me singing, "Ain't Nothin' Gonna Break My Stride, Ain't Nothin' Gonna Slow Me Down" (Matthew Wilder). When I was a mother of three young children surrounded by toys and chaos, you would have heard me singing, "I Will Survive" by Gloria Gaynor. Now, when I'm a middle-aged woman within a stone's throw of the empty nest (and menopause right around the corner), I am humming the phrases of an old hymn: "I need Thee, Oh, I need Thee. Every hour I need Thee."[1] In fact I sang it today as my college-aged kids were driving back to school. Trust me, I am painfully aware of my failures and my need for His saving and sustaining grace.

The reason the Gospel Eight diagram is so fluid is to emphasize the point that we are all *in process.* That means that some days, when my faith is weak and I get sucked into believing the lies, my life will reflect a Gospel Eight where the bottom circle is inflated and *much* larger than the top circle. In practice, I'm living more as an orphan than a child on those days.

Grace is the heartbeat of the gospel.

On other days, when my heart is tender and I am willing to live in relationship and lean on God, I will live more out of my identity in Christ. On those days, the top circle will be *much* larger than the bottom circle.

How I wish I could just erase the bottom portion of this figure eight and never have to deal with that pit!

But the Scriptures show that on this side of heaven the reality of the bottom circle will always be there. As we grow in our faith and His grace sanctifies us, it will grow smaller, reflecting His work in our hearts. Until the world is made new and we are united with Christ, our sin and rebellion will be a constant reminder of our need for a Savior.

The diagram is also fluid in another way. Imagine the diagram animated with motion going in the direction of the arrows. *What propels us forward? What drives you to the cross? What restores your relationship with God? What exposes your unbelief? What pursues you when you choose to go your own way? What rescues you when you are living in that pit?*

Grace.

At the beginning of this book I shared the story of my spiritual unraveling. There was a huge disconnect in my heart between what I knew in my head and what I lived in reality. I understood *a lot* about the gospel, but I was missing one huge, important piece: grace. I didn't get it. In a lot of ways I still don't get it. But I know I need it—desperately. Grace is the heartbeat of the gospel. It's what propels us forward and breathes life and healing into our hearts.

It's funny how God works. Just as I began writing this section about how the cycle works in real life, a friend posted a song on her Facebook page that I had never heard before: "Grace Flows Down" sung by Christy Nockels.[2] It describes Christ's death on the cross by saying, "Grace flows down and covers me." That's true. Grace flows down, *but it also flows around*. It is always pushing me, no matter where I am, back to Jesus.

SWIMMING in the GOSPEL

After a friend of mine realized she had a small view of God and wasn't that excited about her faith, she asked what she could do to expand her view of God. What a great question!

I like to think the answer is to swim in the gospel. Gospel truths are all around us—we just need to open our eyes. I encouraged her to begin by writing down anything that caused her to think differently about God or any experience that helped her see God in a new way. This was important because her "impression" of God had not been based on how He revealed Himself in Scripture, but was an image of Him created out of her personal pain and story.

Glimpses of grace are all around us. You might be reminded

of the gospel by a book you read, a movie you watch, a spectacular sunset, a view from a mountaintop, or even a country song! Echoes of redemption are everywhere, but the primary source for the truth about God is His Word, the Bible.

As God began doing a new work in me, every time I read a passage of Scripture that spoke to idolatry, I put an "I" beside it. I wrote a "J" beside verses about justification and an "A" beside passages about adoption. This step alone caused my senses to wake up and pay attention to what I was learning about the gospel.

> You need friends to point you back to the cross when you forget how loved you are.

I began listening in a new way in church to the songs that we sang, clinging to phrases that pointed me to the gospel. And as the Gospel Eight diagram unfolded in my head, I could see the pattern reflected in passages of Scripture like Psalm 40 and many other passages.

In addition, friends have been a huge part of my journey, and they will be for you too. We were not meant to spend life alone, in isolation. As tempting as it is to pull back, we need each other. We need people in our lives who are willing to speak truth into our hearts. You need friends who will remind you of the gospel and point you back to the cross when you forget just how loved you are. Sometimes your friends will have to fight for your faith when you feel you have none.

I read this quote in a blog post by the creative artist Kevin Marks, and it almost made me stand up and scream, "Yes!"

It is packed with life-giving truth about the importance of living together in community: "Bonhoeffer said that when Christ calls a man he bids him come and die. He never said there wouldn't be brothers and sisters reaching down in joy, arm in arm to start the long, difficult climb out from the grave together."[3] I like this so much because I can actually visualize myself wallowing around in the bottom part of the diagram and friends reaching in and grabbing me and walking with me through the difficult path of surrender.

I have seen this played out in real life. A friend went through a terrible crisis in her marriage. As she emerged on the other side of her pain, she told a group of us that we were like columns that surrounded her during her darkest days, but we were columns covered with pillows that she could lean into when she was too weak to stand. You don't need to walk this journey alone; ask others to walk with you as you fight for faith.

What are you swimming in? Do you feel like you are drowning? Does what you are currently swimming in leave you feeling isolated and numb? Weary and discouraged? Can I be bold and not so gently suggest that you change the hole you are swimming in?

Rather, immerse yourself in the beauty of the gospel, and you will say, as the writer of Hebrews declared, "It is good for our hearts to be strengthened by grace" (Hebrews 13:9).

THE PURPOSE of OUR **ADOPTION**

One thing that all of us have in common since the fall is that we tend to look at everything in terms of how it affects us. It's easy to think everything is all about me, all the time. As a culture we are **absorbed** with ourselves, our children, our work, and our families. But we misunderstand the gospel and the purpose of our salvation if we think it's all about us. We get to enjoy the benefits and blessings of the gospel, but it is definitely not about us!

There's a phrase that rings out over and over again in the Old Testament. It is not always said the same way, but the theme remains: "Then they will know that I am the Lord."

That pretty much sums it up. The purpose of our salvation

and adoption is for us to point others to Christ. John Piper reminds us to "make much of Jesus." Steve Brown encourages us to "smell like Jesus." The bottom line is that we are to live in such a way that God is glorified, we are satisfied, and others are drawn to Him.

Philippians 2:15 encourages us to shine like stars in the universe. Ephesians 1:12–14 describes it like this:

> *In order that we, who were the first to put our hope in Christ, might* ***be for the praise of his glory****. And you also were included in Christ when you heard the message of truth, the gospel of your salvation. When you believed, you were marked in him with a seal, the promised Holy Spirit, who is a deposit guaranteeing our inheritance until the redemption of those who are God's possession—****to the praise of his glory****.* (emphasis mine)

As our hearts are enlarged by faith, the true miracle of our salvation, and the blessing of our adoption, we can't help but respond. **We respond through renewed worship, renewed service, and renewed joy—all for the praise of His glory, not ours.**

It's interesting to me that some people fear that an understanding of the gospel of grace will lead to spiritual apathy and paralysis. I have even been told that this book is dangerous because it is "too much grace." Is "too much grace" even possible? As long as we are giving a true picture of grace, can there be too much? Isn't the greater danger the spiritual ambivalence that comes from a *small* view of grace and the gospel? Can there ever be "too much grace"?

The more I understand and am saturated with grace, the more truly my life will reflect the Father who loves me and the Savior who saved me. I like the way Elyse Fitzpatrick sums up this tension when she says, "Your growth in holiness is firmly bound to your appreciation of the gospel and God's love. Only an appreciation of His love can motivate genuine obedience."[4] Paul put it a little differently in Romans 1:5 when he called people from among the Gentiles to the "obedience that comes from faith." Our faith in what God has done will lead to a transformed life characterized by worship and works. Unless these flow out of an understanding of the gospel of grace, they will be nothing more than sterile acts of service that lead to spiritual burnout and disappointment with God.

One day as I was explaining the Gospel Eight diagram, a woman remarked that she definitely was spinning around in the cycle of living like an orphan, even though she was a believer. She was apathetic and ambivalent about her faith, so she felt disinterested in sharing the gospel. She confessed, "Why would I want to invite anyone to join me? I don't want anyone to have to live like this."

What a great insight! And it brings up the important question: "What are you inviting others into?" If you have a small view of God and live like a spiritual orphan, there really is not a lot to get excited about, is there? But when you are living like a child because God has captured your heart and you are undone by His holiness and humbled by His grace—that is something to celebrate and worth inviting others to join.

Can I just tell you my favorite part of this diagram is the person holding the balloons with outstretched arms? It's an image that speaks volumes: Freedom. Joy. Peace. It's the picture of a person living with a heart full of faith. And it is an *invitation*—to you and to others. Join the party!

Sitting in my kitchen window is a decorative tile given to me by a dear friend before she moved to South Africa. It simply says, "The Lord has done great things for us, and we are filled with joy" (Psalm 126:3). It reminds me that I have tasted and I have seen. I have tasted God's grace and seen it work its way into my heart. He has changed me. Grace continues to drip its way into the parched places of my heart and bring healing.

Today as I was washing dishes, a dishrag hung over the rim of the sink. When I touched it, it felt beyond dry. The rag was so stiff it could have stood up on its corners. It was brittle and unbending. There's no telling what had dried into those threads.

It reminded me how my heart must look when I feel weary and hardened. As I rinsed the rag, it immediately became limp and pliable in my hands. A little water changed everything. Even if I had only added a drip at a time, eventually the rag would have become saturated. The gospel is like that. Sometimes it grabs hold of us in a fury and totally saturates us. At other times, it is just a slow, steady drip pursuing and wooing us back to Him.

Those little "drops" of grace remind me of what I'm like when I am craving something sweet. I start looking for something that will hit the spot and satisfy my craving. A pack of Smarties might be good enough for some people, but that doesn't quite cut it with me. I am on the hunt for chocolate. I don't need a whole bag. *I just need a taste. Just a drop.*

Seems like a silly way to think about grace, but I cannot tell you how many times just a taste, just a drop of His grace in any given situation has been enough to settle my heart and refocus my mind.

The psalmist says, "Taste and see that the Lord is good; blessed is the one who takes refuge in him" (Psalm 34:8).

Take refuge in His love. Soak in the gospel—even if it comes as a slow drip. Let His grace saturate you, and then share it with those around you.

They are craving it, but they might not know it. Yet.

DIGGING *Deeper*

1. Take a moment and in the margin draw a Gospel Eight outline that honestly reflects where you are right now in your relationship with God. Which circle is larger and why?
2. What have been your theme songs during various stages of your life?
3. What does God use to awaken you to the beauty of the gospel?
4. Take a step back and honestly evaluate what you are currently swimming in. *What you "swim in" is a reflection of what you are craving.*
5. Do you need to make an adjustment in your life that would put you on a path to experience more of His grace?
6. If by reading this book you have discovered you have a small view of God, your sin, or the gospel, try keeping a list of the glimpses of grace He brings into your life each day.
7. Ask God to give you a picture of how He can use you in your current situation to make His name great and invite others into relationship with Him.

DRAWING the GOSPEL EIGHT **DIAGRAM**

Now that you understand the diagram, it's time for you to learn to draw it! I won't make you draw the tricky, detailed one. Instead I'll just ask you to draw the simple version I use when I teach. It's so easy to draw, I have drawn it on the back of a receipt and on a napkin at a restaurant.

It doesn't really matter how you draw this diagram, but, if you like step-by-step instructions, here is one suggestion of how it can be done.

CHILD of GOD
Intimacy with God
God is...
I am...
Redeemer
Redeemed
Protector
Safe
Ruler
Under His Control
Comforter
Peaceful
Restoration
Awareness of sin
TRUE REPENTANCE
REST
RESIST
I was...
I am...
Controlled
Bitter
Abused
Angry
Successful
Proud
Misled
Anxious
Isolation
blaming • denial • minimizing
FALSE REPENTANCE
FALSE GODS
work • approval • $$ • family
Awareness of sin
ORPHAN
Isolation from God

- Draw the figure eight and insert the directional arrows and the little dark cross at the bottom of the upper circle.
- Label the outside of the top and bottom circles "Child" and "Orphan" as indicated.
- Label "Awareness of Sin," "Restoration," and "Isolation."
- Label the bottom left curve with "False Repentance" on the inside curve and examples of the types on the outside curve.
- Label the bottom right curve with "False gods" inside the curve and examples of idolatry outside the curve.
- Label the interior of the top circle reflecting our identity in Christ. You can list any attributes of God you choose. You do not have to use the ones I have chosen. You can also fill this circle with more than just the attributes of God and include all the riches of the gospel found throughout Scripture.
- Label the interior of the bottom circle reflecting our identity as spiritual orphans. There is no limit to what this list of descriptions can include. Choose the ones that relate best to your own story, or ones you think will connect with others as you share your diagram. Make sure your list includes more than just negative adjectives. We tend to think of descriptions like "competent" and "independent" as positive traits (which they can be), but those normally positive traits are not helpful when living as an orphan. So be sure to include those as well.

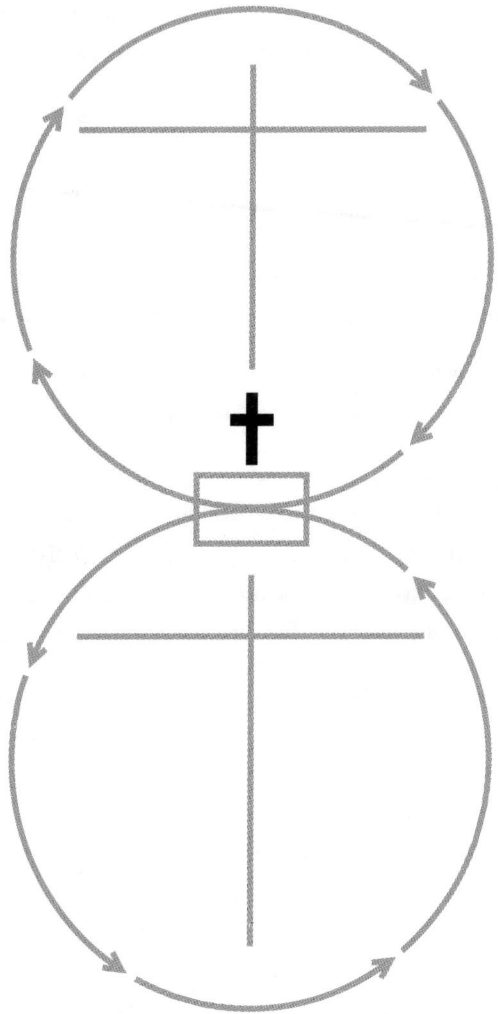

For additional copies, visit www.CravingGrace.org.

The only hard part about drawing this is remembering it! So practice it enough times that you can share it should God give you the opportunity. You can start with the outline provided here. Also, remember to practice talking through it a few times out loud so that you can share it from your heart.

Not long after my friend Deb learned about the Gospel Eight, she had lunch with a friend who was battling breast cancer. As they talked, Deb realized that, for her friend, the cancer diagnosis had been like a tsunami to her sense of identity. So Deb shared the diagram with her. A week later she read this on her friend's blog, *Pilgrims Pathway—Our Journey Together with Him.*

> *Per dear Deb's doodle drawing lesson—I will choose to live as the greatly blessed child of God that I am, not a spiritual orphan. He is my Forgiver: I confess my sin to Him and I am forgiven. He is my Redeemer: I am redeemed by the blood of the Lamb. He is my Savior: I am saved through simple faith. He is my Deliverer: I am delivered from every bondage to sin . . . delivered from eternal death/separation from Him, delivered from fear and doubt. He is my Provider, and I am well provided for by Him in every way. He is my Defender: I am defended. He is the Lover of my soul: I am loved with an everlasting love. He is my Healer, and I can trust Him to heal me if that is best. (Oh Lord, is it Your best to heal me of cancer, the invisible tourniquet sensation on my arm, the side effects/damage done from the chemo? I wish healing me would be Your very best! I pray so. Please help me to trust and*

rest in You and Your will, no matter what.) I know my absolute ultimate "perfect" healing will be a new body in heaven, worshiping Him there forever, just not sure about the here and now on earth part. Because of my position in Christ, I do not have to "live as an orphan" or give in to bitterness, loneliness, a controlling nature, fear, doubt, blaming others, broken relationships, or anger OR ANY OTHER SUCH THING. God has MUCH better for me! Thank You, Lord and Deb, for the "doodle drawing lesson" spelling this out for me!

What a great picture of God's truth and grace seeping into the cracked places of a heart and bringing healing! All because Deb shared a bit of truth and grace with a hurting friend. *Don't be surprised* if God puts someone in your path who needs to hear the truth of God's grace embedded in this diagram. *Don't be afraid* to scribble it on whatever is handy. **Then be amazed when God does what only God can do!**

STARTING A NEW **LIFE**

If reading this book and studying the diagram has prompted you to consider Jesus for the first time, I'd like to share what your next steps might be. Maybe you feel separated from God, like you are spinning around in the bottom circle with no one who really cares. There's hope. The solution in moving toward a relationship with God begins with taking a long look in the mirror, at the broken and messy places of your heart, then looking up at the cross.

Faith in Christ involves three things: admit, believe, and confess.

***Admit* that you are a sinner—not** just that you sin, but that your heart is tainted with sin that corrupts your entire being. Your sin separates you from God. He is holy and hates sin. That's why He had to punish His only Son. Someone had to pay for your sin.

Believe that outside of Christ there is no solution, no forgiveness, no lasting peace. **Believe** Christ died for your sin and that not only can He wipe your slate clean through the cross, but He gives you His slate! He is not going to judge you for all the wrong things you do. Instead He will give you the righteousness Jesus earned by living a perfect life. When you trust Him to take away your sin, He sees you as clothed in the beauty and perfection of Christ.

Confess your need for a Savior and ask God to forgive you. Trust in Christ to be your Deliverer and look to what Jesus has done for you on the cross. God will forgive you and restore you as His child.

This is the doorway of the gospel. If you have taken these steps, welcome to the family! You've begun a relationship with God. Ahead of you is a new journey of walking with God through ups and downs and twists and turns. But on the path is every promise, every truth about God, every spiritual blessing offered to His children! You have been given a new identity as His child, and you will forever be a part of His family. Nothing can separate you from the love of God.

As you begin this relationship with God, you will want to surround yourself with people who can encourage you and equip you along the way. Find a community of believers where you can grow in your new faith. Enjoy the blessings of adoption and ***remember*** the gospel! **Even as you continue to sin and struggle with doubt and unbelief, remember the solution is always the same: run to the cross. It changes everything!**

USING THIS BOOK with a **GROUP**

There are a couple of ways you can use this book with a small group.

The standard way would be for members to read a section ahead of time and be prepared to share their thoughts and discuss the *Digging Deeper* questions together.

An alternative would be to read the section together, either out loud or silently, when you meet. The sections are not that long and would only take a few minutes to read. The advantage of this method is that everyone is literally "on the same page" and prepared. Then you can move through a discussion and answer the *Digging Deeper* questions.

Some of you are teachers and will want to use this material

as a springboard to leading your own study. It is pretty obvious that there is still much to be shared about each of the topics covered in this book. **Remember, the book's purpose is to start the conversation!** So as a teacher you could easily expand on any of the topics and add your own stories, Scriptures, and illustrations.

You might want to study this book together while at the same time reading *From Fear to Freedom* by Rose Marie Miller, *The Transforming Power of the Gospel* by Jerry Bridges, or any other gospel-centered resource!

The questions at the end of each section are simply meant as a guide for discussion. I provided more questions than you will likely be able to cover during a session. As a leader you might want to select a few that seem appropriate for your group. For additional resources to share with your group, copies of charts, and videos explaining the diagram, visit cravinggrace.org.

However you choose to pursue this, I pray it will propel you forward in your journey into experiencing the richness of the gospel.

RECOMMENDED **READING**

The list below includes titles that have had an amazing impact on my journey in learning to believe and apply the gospel to my life. If you are looking to grow, then dive into these life-changing books. Ones marked with an asterisk make an especially natural follow-up to *Craving Grace.* Grab a friend and grow together!

Bold Love, Dan Allender (NavPress)
Surrender to Love, David G. Benner (InterVarsity Press)
Transforming Grace, Jerry Bridges (NavPress)*
Trusting God Even When Life Hurts, Jerry Bridges (NavPress)
The Transforming Power of the Gospel, Jerry Bridges (NavPress)
Because He Loves Me, Elyse Fitzpatrick (Crossway)*
Comforts from the Cross, Elyse Fitzpatrick (Crossway)
Counsel from the Cross, Elyse Fitzpatrick (Crossway)
Bravehearts: Unlocking the Courage to Love with Abandon, Sharon Hersch (WaterBrook)
Counterfeit Gods, Tim Keller (Dutton)

**Galatians for You*, Tim Keller (The Good Book Company)
A Praying Life, Paul E. Miller (NavPress)
**From Fear to Freedom*, Rose Marie Miller (WaterBrook)
Desiring God, John Piper (Multnomah)
Future Grace, John Piper (Multnomah)
Strong Women, Soft Hearts, Paula Rinehart (Word)
Everyday Prayers, Scotty Smith, devotional (Baker Books)
Objects of His Affection, Scotty Smith (Howard)
A Gospel Primer, Milton Vincent, devotional (Focus)
Addictions: A Banquet in the Grave, Edward T. Welch (Presbyterian & Reformed)

"True Spirituality: The Transforming Power of the Gospel," Steve Childers, Global Church Advancement, www.gca.cc.

NOTES

PREFACE: Why This Book?

1. Jerry Bridges, "The Pursuit of Holiness: An Interview," *Tabletalk* magazine from Ligonier Ministries and R. C. Sproul. www.ligonier.org.
2. "Come, Thou Fount of Every Blessing," a hymn by Robert Robinson, 1757.

CHAPTER 1: The Gospel Every Day

1. Please note that I am not using the term *orphan* to disparage or belittle those who have actually lost their parents. I'm referencing the literary/popular definition as those who are forced to live on their own without anyone to look out for them.
2. Paul David Tripp, *Whiter than Snow: Meditations on Sin and Mercy* (Wheaton, IL: Crossway, 2008), 32.

CHAPTER 2: Repentance: A Sweet Gift

1. Dan Allender, *The Wounded Heart* (Colorado Springs: NavPress, 1990), 202.
2. Tripp, *Whiter than Snow*, 41.

CHAPTER 3: Restoration of Relationship

1. There are several useful lists of diagnostic questions for discovering your idols. Google search *How do I discover my idols?* to find further resources.

2. Elyse Fitzpatrick, *Comforts from the Cross: Celebrating the Gospel One Day at a Time* (Wheaton, IL: Crossway, 1009), 116.

3. Timothy J. Keller, *Counterfeit Gods: The Empty Promises of Money, Sex, and Power, and the Only Hope That Matters* (New York: Dutton, 2009), xvii.

4. Steve Childers, "True Spirituality: The Transforming Power of the Gospel," Global Church Advancement, www.gca.cc.

CHAPTER 4: Renewed Identity: Child vs. Orphan

1. J. I. Packer, *Knowing God* (Downers Grove, IL: InterVarsity Press, 1993), 187–188.

2. For additional copies of the Orphan vs. Child chart, visit www.Craving Grace.org.

CHAPTER 5: Responding to Sin

1. Rose Marie Miller, *From Fear to Freedom* (Colorado Springs: Water-Brook, 1994), 5.

CHAPTER 7: Real Life and the Cycle of Grace

1. "I Need Thee Every Hour," Annie S. Hawks, 1872.

2. David E. Bell, Louie Giglio, Rod Padgett, "Grace Flows Down," *Passion: One Day Live* (Sparrow, 2000).

3. Kevin Marks, quoted by Bonnie Gray, "Touching the Artistic Life You've Hidden Deep Inside," May 28, 2013, www.incourage.me.

4. Elyse Fitzpatrick, *Because He Loves Me: How Christ Transforms Our Daily Life* (Wheaton, IL: Crossway, 2008), 109.

ABOUT THE **AUTHOR**

Ruthie Delk grew up in Belgium and graduated from Furman University in Greenville, South Carolina, with a degree in special education. She and her husband, David, live in Orlando, Florida, where he is president of Man in the Mirror. David and Ruthie have three children. She is passionate about helping women embrace the gospel in such a way that it captures their hearts and not just their minds. She enjoys watching movies, drinking sweet tea, riding her bike, and eating any assortment of cheap chocolates.

ABOUT THE GOSPEL EIGHT DIAGRAM

The original Gospel Eight diagram came to life through an incredible doodle that my friend Deb McCrary drew after a Craving Grace bible study. She used to feel guilty about doodling while taking notes—but not anymore! I am deeply grateful for her compulsive doodling and that I can call her my friend. I am especially thankful for Matt Smartt and Spencer Grahl at Smartt Guys design for catching the vision and developing such a polished version for the book.

CravingGrace.org

Find additional resources for your own journey or ministry to women at CravingGrace.org. You can download copies of the charts used in this book or purchase ten-packs of laminated Gospel Eight diagrams. A brief video describing the Gospel Eight diagram, as well as additional teaching videos are also available.

Find us on Facebook at Craving Grace. LIKE our page for encouraging quotes, video clips, and music that will keep you swimming in the gospel.

ACKNOWLEDGMENTS

This book reflects a group effort. The contents have been shaped by so many people that their fingerprints are literally all over these pages—from dear friends and Bible study groups to a phone call with a stranger.

I am grateful for the pastors from University Presbyterian Church who have given me a steady diet of gospel-centered preaching through the years. I am especially grateful for Pastor Mark Bates and his wife, Tricia, who helped me make sense of my struggles in the early days of UPC.

To the co-op moms, Karen, Becky, Alisa, Deb, and Renee: You have been faithful friends, and I laugh when I think how we have literally talked circles around all of these truths! Thanks for helping me in my journey and being such an encouragement. So glad we get to do life together.

Thanks to the CC Smart Mama Bible Study from the summer of 2011 for forcing me to write it all down and to dear friends Johnny and Christy LaLonde, who in one evening turned a circle with exit ramps into a figure eight. Pure genius!

I am especially grateful to Deb McCrary for using her doodling to capture the heart of the Gospel Eight diagram. You brought it to life, and this book would not exist without it! I am so thankful you took "Stop doodling" off your New Year's Resolutions list. You have a gift. Keep doodling!

Finally, to my amazing husband, David, and children, Ryan, Sarah, and Kyle: You are with me on the days when I am living like an orphan and on the days when I am struggling to live like His child. You've seen it all (and sometimes it's pretty ugly), yet you still love me. Thank you!

AN ANCHOR FOR THE SOUL

978-0-8024-1536-3

An Anchor for the Soul is written with doubters, seekers, and skeptics in mind. In a clear, straightforward presentation, he answers questions such as: What is God like? How can I know Him? Who is Jesus and what did He do?

His Word In My Heart

978-0-8024-0964-5

We daily strive without doing the most important thing, the best thing — putting God's Word in our hearts and minds. And then we wonder why — Why am I not growing? Why do I still struggle with this same sin? Why is my family faltering?

The good news is *YOU* can do it. In this updated classic, Janet Pope will share practical tips and strategies — including how to harness technology — to enable you to start memorizing the living Word today.

Also available as an ebook

From the Word to Life

www.MoodyPublishers.com

Pour yourself a cup of coffee and enjoy **Java with Juli**, a new podcast by host and clinical psychologist Dr. Juli Slattery. From the cozy setting of a coffee shop, Juli offers a woman's perspective on intimacy and converses with guests about the challenges of being a contemporary Christian woman.

www.moodyradio.org/javawithjuli

*From the Word **to Life***